A Place to Live

By

Abraham Lincoln

June 2006

My birthplace, Gordon, Ohio, was thought to be the place to live in Darke County, Ohio. It was carved out of a vast wilderness that was ripe with wolves, bear and screaming panthers. Newspaper columns proclaimed its potential and how it would become a big town—larger than Arcanum and rivaling Greenville, the county seat. It had a new school and church, and several businesses with products and services that were widely distributed by the new railroad. The Ohio Pure Food Company, in Gordon, was famous for its chocolate and advertised: *"Townsend's Chocolate are good enough for queens, preachers and sweethearts."* This was a small village with a large steam sawmill that employed many people cutting local hardwoods into saleable lumber. Barrel hoops were made here by coopers who moved into town from as far away as Piqua. Many families in Gordon kept boarders—people who lived in private homes and worked in local industry. The families in this book lived in Gordon from the year 1848 to 1998.

A Place to Live

By

Abraham Lincoln

June 2006

— • —

Contents

The Land Grants

A Land Grant document, signed by President John Quincy Adams, in 1825, granted the "East Half of the North Quarter of Section Thirty-five in Township Eight of Range Three East" containing 80 acres, "more or less" to Jonas Albright of Preble County. Jonas Albright, a Revolutionary War soldier, was paid for his services with this grant of land.

Jonas Albright and his wife, Margaret, of Eaton, Ohio, sold their Eastern Section of Land to Jacob Tilman, in 1832 for the sum of two hundred and thirty-seven dollars and fifty-cents.

In 1832, President Andrew Jackson signed a land grant to one Jacob Emmons of Darke County, Ohio for the "West Half of the North Quarter of Section Thirty-six in Township Eight of Range Three East containing 80 acres, more or less."

Jacob Emmons sold his Western Section of Land to Philip and Elizabeth Gordon in 1839 for the sum of one thousand five-hundred dollars -- a princely sum in those days, and considerably more than Tilman paid for the Eastern Section.

It Was a Wilderness

The landmass occupied by the boundary of a state we call "Ohio" consisted of 26 millions of acres of forests and meadows. One hundred and twenty varieties of trees are native to this landmass. James Elliott recorded remarks about land and trees during his trip to Fort Greene Ville in 1795 — the year the Treaty of Greene Ville was signed.

"This afternoon I took a walk, accompanied by two of my fellow soldiers, into the woods west of the cantonment. In the course of our perambulations, we observed and accurately examined a huge sycamore tree, which, at a few inches from the ground, measured between 40 and 50 feet in circumference. From this enormous trunk proceeded seven considerable branches, four of which could be called large trees in the northern states."

The eastern part of the township was mostly swampland. It had large stands of timber that was valued by early settlers. In the vicinity of Gordon were large stands of hickory and this wood was used for barrel hoops. Mary [Hillard] Clark's husband, James, moved to Gordon because he was a maker of barrel hoops and worked in one of the town's first industries -- a "cooperage."

The abundance of moisture explains the grand forests that covered primitive Darke County. Rooted in naturally rich soil, the trees were fed by an unfailing supply of water and moisture from the springs and streams. There were trees everywhere and few meadows or prairies to be found in the county. Beautiful groves of fine oaks were along the ridges, skirting the creek prairies and in level wet places, soft maple grew in abundance as in Butler Township. The hard sugar maple predominated to the delight of the Indians and the pioneers. Beech groves were found in a few places, mostly in the southern and western parts of the county and on the ridges in the northern part. Along the streams grew giant white bole sycamores, the stately American Elm, the graceful linden and the verdant willow.

The forest was also filled with ash, shagbark hickory, and black walnut. There was yellow poplar, buckeye, locust, cottonwood, slippery elm, butternut, black cherry, mulberry, coffee berry, silver maple and dogwood, red bud, black-haw, red-haw, papaw and a larger variety of shrubbery, which often made an almost impenetrable growth of underbrush dotted with sumac, hazelnut, blackberry and raspberry.

In 1883, an oak was cut down in German Township that measured six feet across the stump and contained over five hundred annual rings of growth. It was 109 years of age when Columbus discovered America. In 1902 a large poplar tree fell to the ground in western Ohio and was purchased by E. L. Fields of Union City, Indiana. It measured six feet across the stump and was eighteen feet in circumference and was 74 feet to the first limb. This tree, by a careful count of the growth rings, was over 400 years old. A large and rare specimen of the coffee berry tree stood below Fort Jefferson on the northwest part of section 34, Neave Township. For many years it was a notable landmark standing at the fork of the old trails — St. Clair's trace and the one leading to Fort Black (New Madison). After the top was shattered by winds the trunk was cut down. The trunk was about four feet across and it is recorded as the largest specimen of this variety in the United States. A white oak was felled on section 18, Neave Township that measured about seven feet in diameter. In Twin Township, early settlers felled a Burr Oak about seven feet in diameter.

The variety of wildlife was hard for us to imagine. Deer supplied many of the early settlers with meat. Each year thousands of deer hams were delivered down river to Cincinnati and beyond. The countryside was filled with bears, wolves, foxes, raccoons, woodchucks, opossums, skunks and squirrels. There were turkeys, geese, ducks, partridges and pigeons. Eagles and turkey buzzards were frequently seen. Owls and hawks were common throughout the landmass we call Ohio.

The great forest bison roamed through the meadows and forest. Slightly darker and smaller than their cousins, they were common but not as plentiful as the plains buffalo. Christopher Gist called them "buffaloes" and remarked how they roamed throughout the forest and meadows. At the time Daniel Boone came to the Kentucky lands, and when the while settlers began coming through the mountains to the Ohio Valley, herds of buffalo and elk roamed the forests and prairies of Tennessee, Kentucky and all north of the Ohio River to the Mississippi.

In 1780 when General Clarke's expedition against the Indian village on the Mad River, seventeen miles above Dayton, had recrossed the Ohio, being low on provisions, a buffalo was killed on Licking River. Two buffalo were killed swimming the Ohio River at the mouth of the Big Miami on November 4, 1787.

In 1788, in a letter written at Marietta, to a friend in Massachusetts, the writer said, "We have seen twenty buffalo in a drove and deer are as plenty as sheep with you; beaver and otter are abundant."

By 1795 the buffalo and the elk had entirely disappeared from the country east of the Wabash.

Wolves, panthers and wild cats were especially annoying to the settlers. Rewards were paid for every wolf scalp brought-in and thousands were destroyed. Squirrels ate ripening grain and thousands were shot every year. Several counties paid one-third of a cent for a squirrel scalp with ears and later insisted that part of their taxes be paid in squirrel scalps.

Pigeons were a genuine pest not only because they ate large amounts of ripe grain, but also because the sheer numbers deposited enormous amounts of slimy muck on the land. Their weight alone, when roosting, often broke strong oak tree limbs. John Bradbury records that he discovered pigeons in the woods and exchanged his rifle for a fowling piece and in a few hours killed 271 pigeons. There were so many pigeons that the sun would be blacked out when a flock passed overhead. It is hard to imagine that such numbers could be destroyed, but the last passenger pigeon is stuffed and on display at the zoo in Cincinnati.

The Indians who lived in this state or who passed through it lived a simple life. The forest provided them with all their needs, from animal skins for clothing, food and shelter, to patches of ground where they grew corn, beans and melons. They owned nothing but claimed "rights" to hunting and camping grounds. They were a stoic people, insensible to pain, suffering, fatigue and physical exposure. They were also eloquent in self-expression and speech to assemblies. Their memories were without faults and their intellect was always a marvel to the whites that met them in council. The few traces or trails through the forest were in constant use and the streams were used by Indians in their canoes. It was impossible to move large wagons and armies of men through the forest until roads were cut through and the underbrush was cleared away.

Major General Arthur St. Clair, in 1791, cut a road about 9 – 12 feet wide, from Fort Hamilton through the wilderness and established forts like Fort Jefferson. He said that progress was slow and the army had only advanced twenty miles in five days (4th to 9th of October). The following day an open beech country was reached (near Eaton, Ohio) and about eight miles was made. The following afternoon the army reached the wet prairie (Maple Swamp near present Castine, Ohio) at the headwaters of Twin Creek, some thirty-eight miles from Fort Hamilton. After finding a passage around the swamp, the army struck a well-worn Indian trail that led through and avoided the wet places. It was the morning of the 13th of October when St. Clair selected a site for a fort of deposit in the graveled and rolling hills and called it Fort Jefferson.

Captain Daniel Bradley describes the building of Fort Jefferson. He writes, "October 14th we continue on this ground. A large party is imploy'd in falling timber for the purpose of building a fortification. 15, 16, 17, 18th remain on this ground 200 men constantly imployed building a fort, The army was this day reduced to one day provision but pack horses are now coming in with flour. I suppose four or five days, whether we get more when that's gone I know not.

"Deer & bear are so plenty here it is common for them to run through our camp sometimes knock down tents, men, etc. The last three or four days have been very wet, bad weather."

"October 19th — this morning by a gen'l order we are reduced to half a lb. flour per day in consequence of failure on the part of the contractor. We have got the fort high enough & now begin to lay the rafters. It falls to Capt. Shaylor's and my lot to be stationed at this garrison, called FORT JEFFERSON, with about 120 invalids which we take possession on this day."

After the fort was completed, the army moved on northward following an Indian trail on the east side of the prairie. To the north about six miles they found an excellent campsite on elevated ground with a wide creek in front of their campsite (Greenville, Ohio).

General Wayne, in 1793, cut the same road through the same area that St. Clair had cut two years earlier. Wayne widened it to forty feet and cleared the underbrush.

On July 28, 1795, James Elliot made an excursion into the wilderness and wandered southwesterly into the prairie that begins at the confluence of Greenville Creek and Mud Creek. "I came upon a beautiful prairie, about half a mile in breadth, and many miles in length. A party of six soldiers, employed in making hay, had pitched their tents on what is called an upland, which is a small eminence in the prairie, covered with trees and bushes." He said, "Blackberries, in astonishing quantities, abound in the charming groves on the margins of the prairies; also an abundance of wild plums."

Elliot says a "Large, extensive, verdant prairie — or natural meadow, covered with grass and innumeral flowers, without a tree or bush, as far as the eye can reach, except an occasional small grove, or thicket; which may be compared to a small island in the midst of an immense ocean. The jonquils, the primrose, the cowslip, the daisy, the violet, the hyacinth, and other aromatics, conspire to beautify the prospect and enhance the fragrance of the breezes, which constantly flow on the meadow. A species of wild onion grows spontaneously here in incredible quantites, equally good, though not quite so ransid as the onion of New England; and make as palatable salads as were ever tasted."

Elliot describes animals in the area: "The herds of deer and buffalo are literally innumerable. Although the troops at Greenville hunted daily in the vicinity of that place, yet, I have frequently started deer with half a mile of camp. Wolves are numerous, as are foxes, opossums, rabbits, raccoons, polecats, squirrels, etc., and the water abound with beavers, minks, otters, and other amphibious animals."

On some interest is the statement that supplies were received from headquarters at Fort Washington (Cincinnati) by boat, no doubt by way of the Great Miami and Stillwater Rivers and Greenville Creek. This suggests that these streams retained their water more fully before the heavy forest were cut down and the cities and large factories diverted their waters for their own convenience. These conjectures are fortified by the statement that Colonel Sargent made indicating that Greenville Creek was forty feet wide when St. Clair's army arrived in 1791. Other early settler accounts also tell how clear the waters of stream were. It is recorded that you could see fish in the streams and the bottom of still rivers. High water or floods didn't seem to occur as often and even then the water was clear except around forts and gardens that had exposed soil close to the water.

This land was truly a wilderness when Philip Gordon and his family decided to leave New Jersey and move to Ohio. His son-in-law, David Lair, kept a daily record of their journey and that is presented below with the original spelling and punctuation.

Philip Gordon and Family Moves to Ohio

On the 20th day of May 1839, Philip Gordon left his ancestral home in New Jersey (Hunterdon County) to become a pioneer settler in what was then "The Far West" State of Ohio. With him came Elizabeth [Harden] Gordon, his wife, his sons, Andrew and Henry, David and Sarah [Gordon] Lair (their daughter and son-in-law), and Amie Lair, and Mary Gordon, an unmarried daughter, who afterwards became Mrs. John Karr and resided one mile east of Gordon, Ohio.

The party was equipped with covered wagons drawn by horses and their journey took two weeks. The daily progress was recorded by David Lair and transcribed in 1929 by Franklin S. Gordon, the grandson of Philip Gordon. The manuscript was preserved in the family Bible of Mrs. John Karr.

Left New Jersey May 20th, 1839 and landed in Philadelphia 42 miles the 21st.

Left Philadelphia passed into Delaware County made 12 miles the 22nd.

Passed Chester, County Town of Chester County, cross the East and West Brandywine and made 26 miles the 23rd.

Passed Strassburg rail road and stayed at Mill Port, made 26 miles the 24.

Passed Lancaster County Town of Lancaster County, crossed the Susquehanna at Columbia, stayed at Little York, County Town of York County. Made 25 mile the 25th.

Past Abbotsville, stayed at Gettysburg County Town of Adams County made 28 miles the 26th.

Passed Saint Loudin and stayed on top of the North Mountain. Made 18 miles the 28th.

Passed McConnelstown, crossed Scrub Ridge, passed Licking Green crossed Sideling Hill and stayed on Rays Hill. Made 20 miles the 29th.

Passed Bloody Run crossed the Juniatta three times, passed Bedford County Town of Bedford County, stayed where the roads fork for

Wheeling and Pittsburg. Made 23 miles the 30th.

Took the Glade road cross Dry Ridge and stayed on the top of the Alleghany Mountains. Made 21 miles the 31st.

Passed Somersett County Town of Somersett County, stayed on Laurel Hill. Made 30 miles the first of June.

Passed Bennegall in the south corner of Fayette County, passed Chestnut Ridge, passed Mount Pleasant in Westmoreland County. Made 24 miles June 2nd.

Passed through the south corner of Alleghany County, crossed the Monongahela river at Monongahela City, made 27 miles June 3rd.

Passed Washington, County Town of Washington County and took the National Road. Passed West Alexandria and stayed in the State of Virginia, Ohio County (now West Virginia). Made 29 miles June 4th.

Passed Triadelphia and landed in Wheeling at noon. At two oclock cross the Ohio River, passed through St Clairsville, County Town of Balmont County. Made 25 miles June 5th.

Passed Morristown, Fairview, Bricktown and Washington. Made 31 miles June 6th.

Passed Cambridge County Town of Guernsey County, Norwich and Concord and stayed at Zanesville County Town of Muskingum County. Made 31 miles June 7th.

Crossed the Muskingum River, passed Mt. Sterling, Brownsville, Lynnville and cross the Ohio Canal at Hebron, Licking County. Made 33 miles June 8th.

Passed Reynoldsburg, stayed at Pleasant Ridge. Made 19 miles June 9th.

Passed Columbus, County Town of Franklin County and Capitol of the State crossed the Scioto River, passed Jefferson in Madison County, Lafayette and Somerford. Made 33 miles June 10th.

Passed Springfield, County Town of Clarke County, stayed at

Fairfield in Greene County. Made 27 miles June 11th.

Passed Dayton, County Town of Montgomery County and landed in Alexanderville at noon June 12th.

During the temporary halt at Alexanderville one of the children of David and Sarah Lair died and was buried there.

The next move was to Darke County where they established the home where they lived for many years and at their death were buried in the burial ground at Gordon, Ohio, which is a part of the farm which Philip Gordon originally bought.

Philip Gordon was Justice of the Peace for a number of years and when the Dayton and Union Rail Road was built they named the station Gordon in his honor.

In The Beginning

Philip Gordon's land that he transformed into a farm was deep black soil that would produce any crop that might be planted in it.

The entire tract was covered with a heavy growth of walnut, oak, hickory and other timber which Philip proceeded to cut down to make room for housing his family and shelter for his stock. The house he built is still standing but has been made modern in many ways. The Michael Stump family presently owns the farm.

There was no lack of fresh meat in the area, as it seemed to be alive with deer and turkeys. Flour could be milled at nearby Ithaca, a five-mile horseback ride.

Philip built a Baptist church on his property and established the Gordon Cemetery on his land. His son-in-law, David Lair who had accompanied him in covered wagons from New Jersey, helped in building the church and David was also instrumental in having the town of Gordon platted in 1849.

Gordon Station and the Hamlet of Gordon was Platted

The original survey for the town reads as follows: "The Town of Gordon is laid out in the North part of the East half of the North East quarter of Section 35 in Township Eight of Range 3 East. The Streets of said Town run North North & South and East and West crossing at right angles, the lots are numbered consecutively from 1 to 27 and are 1 chain and 25 links in front and 2 chains deep except fractional Lot 27 the length of the boundaries of which are designated on the plat the width of the several streets is shown on that. a stone is set at the N. W. corner of Lot 21 which bears from the N. W. corner of said half quarter of 26 35' & 56 links October 17th., 1849. John Wharry, Sur. Darke County Ohio.

"To all to whom these presents shall come.

"Know ye that I David Lair have laid and established the Town of Gordon in the County of Darke and State of Ohio, conformally to the within plat and notes thereof, signed by the surveyor of said County.

"In witness I have hereto set my hand and seal the 17th of October A. D. 1849. signed David Lair. Executed in the presence of, signed John G. Hutten, signed John Wharry."

A railroad was surveyed and built near the farm. A station house was built there and it was named "Gordon" in appreciation for the many services Philip Gordon provided. The small Gordon Station Building was still standing and in use into the 1960s. Over the years, the small building housed the ticket agent and post office, and it was used as a home for the Blue Ribbon Creamery.

During the 1930s and 1940s, the station was the coal office of George Myers. The building became a private home for Norma [Ballengee] Goins and her two children in the 1940s while her husband, Roy, was serving in the Army in Germany, during the Second World War.

At this time (1849) the railroad was called the "Cincinnati & Miami Rail Road" and is shown on the map of Gordon. One hundred years later, or on a 1949 map, the railroad is labeled "B&O Railroad." An 1888 map shows the railroad called D & U R R a name we shortened to D&U. It is not known if the railroad had been built to and through Arcanum, at that time, but a 1911 map shows the line was through the town of Arcanum It was through Arcanum by 1853). The railroad is still the Cincinnati and Miami on the 1857 map of Gordon. The 1875 map indicates the railroad name was changed to "Dayton and Union Railroad."

The town of Gordon was laid out in 1849, and my copy of the original Plat of the town of Gordon, Darke County, Ohio, reveals a planned community of 27 Lots. Residents of the community speculated in newspaper accounts that they expected that Gordon would grow and become the dominant town in southern Darke County. It had a great location being considerably closer to Dayton, and there were numerous businesses expanding operations in town.

At that time, North Street was merely a connecting street between Main, East and West Streets. There was no road east or west of town where State Route 722 is today.

Main Street was "1 chain wide," and East Street and West Streets were "50 links wide." North Street was also 50 links wide and Perry and Centre (note spelling) were 1 chain wide.

Gordon was incorporated on December 28, 1899. The legal incorporation document is still in the possession of a resident, Charles Rauscher, of North Street.

My copy of a 1910 map shows the railroad was named the "Dayton and Union" and it was called the "D&U" when I lived there. In the 1930s and 1940s the D&U ran twice each day between Dayton, Ohio and Union City, Ohio/Indiana carrying both freight and passengers.

I was born in 1934, but I distinctly remember my mother calling me to come and see the "last passenger train to pass through Gordon." I remember the people waving and the flags on the train, but I was too young to know what the date was.

An Eyewitness—Arcanum and the D&U Railroad

Mrs. McLeod visited Miss Mattie Ivester of Arcanum, Ohio when she was 92 years of age in1919. A newspaper article gives an interesting account of the area and how it was then to ride the railroad passenger trains.

She remembers the early days of Arcanum when only five families lived there. Her first husband, Miller Davis, was a brother to Mrs. George Ivester, mother of Mattie J. Ivester. Mr. Davis died in 1867 and in 1885, Diadame married Mr. George McLeod of Pleasant Mills, Indiana.

Mrs. McLeod originally moved to Arcanum with her first husband in 1851, before the railroad was built through town. The other families residing in Arcanum then were Sam Smith who owned a small store. Sam was a brother of John Smith, who was the father of M. M. Smith and L. H. Smith. William Gunder and his family resided in a house standing several yards west of the Ivester home (A great, great, grandson now lives in a house located on the original site). William Gunder laid out the town of Arcanum in 1849.

Mr. Bolen kept a hotel in Arcanum and Mahlon Floyd and his family made up the total population of Arcanum in 1851 according to Mrs. McLeod. Her husband, Miller Davis, was the town blacksmith.

Mrs. McLeod remembers that when she arrived in Arcanum, everything was swamp and that when she visited the neighbors, she had to walk from log to log to keep out of the mossy green water. She remembers that Philip Albright came to church and used a ten foot pole to vault from one log to the next.

People thought the railroad would be too expensive, but the first night the workmen who were building the railroad arrived in town, her home caught on fire and 52 of the railroad workers helped to extinguish it. The railroad was completed through town in 1852 and she made a trip to Dayton on it the following year (1853). She remembers the water covered the cross ties in many places on the way to Dayton.

The Electric Railway

J. B. Lowes and J. B. Feight, Petitioners, petitioned Darke County for a franchise to construct and maintain a right of way for the electric railway which was known as the "D & N" electric railway.

There were a number of conditions imposed on the new railway company when the petition was granted. One was that the train would not be permitted to travel faster than 40 miles per hour or the company would risk losing the franchise.

My father switched from riding the passenger train to his place of work for Dayton Power and Light Company's substation near Taylorsville, to riding the faster and cheaper "traction cars." My father often told me that the traction used to "fly" down the tracks at speeds near 100 miles per hour.

The speedy electric traction was the cheapest way to travel in the area for many years. The thing that really doomed the electric train was the automobile and the competition for freight from the struggling D&U railroad.

Traction Shuts Down and Rails Removed

Gerald Van Pelt, son of Dr. and Mrs. Van Pelt, said the rails were removed in 1926. The company enlarged the turn on East and North Streets and used a switch engine and flat car to remove the rails. The railroad ties were not removed at the same time. Gerald recalls that his father, had to place some stitches to close a wound of an injured worker named "Sensenbaugh" (The Sensenbaughs lived just west of town on a farm). Helen [Flory] Gentner suggested to me that it was probably *Archie* Sensenbaugh.

Mrs. Knick who lives on the lot where the O'Dell livery stable once stood and where the traction line was located, has found electric railroad spikes while digging in her flower beds. When she learned that I was writing a book about Kids from Gordon, she brought me one of her most recent finds. These spikes are smaller versions of the regular railroad spikes.

Gordon Schools

An 1857 map of Gordon, that I have, shows a "new school" beside the Baptist Church beside the Philip Gordon Cemetery, and within the town (corporation) limits. This was the original school that Philip Gordon and his son-in-law David Lair had built using logs cut on the Gordon farm. The Baptist Church was also constructed on the same lot next to the cemetery.

I went to our country school at Gordon. The official school name was Nealeigh #1, but we just called it "Gordon." It was located in the country west of town. Miss Beatrice Brown was my teacher and the teacher of several generations of 'Kids From Gordon.' She taught all eight grades in one room

In 1994 I walked into my office and noticed a 1944 Gordon School photograph on the wall. I stopped to look at the familiar faces, from fifty years earlier, and wondered where the kids were. Miss Brown had passed on and so had a couple of boys, but I was not sure about the rest. And I began my search for Kids from Gordon.

The Gordon School Kids Reunion of 1995

I began to look for the kids in the school picture. Using the telephone, the computer, and lots of letters led to my finding the 23 kids in the school photograph. Miss Brown was deceased as was Gerald Fisher and Dick Harleman. After finding them I began to search for "all" who ever went to school at Gordon, and finally I searched for those who once lived in Gordon between the early 1800s and when I left town in the 1960s. I found 146, scattered all over the country, and I found numerous relatives.

The oldest 'kid' was then Alma Barklow who was 104 years of age in 1994 — she had attended the same school.

I wrote a book about the 'Kids from Gordon' and we had a reunion at the school on Sunday afternoon, June 25, 1995.

Over 100 kids and their friends showed up. Some came from as far away as California (Roberta [Mowry] Ridgeway), Arizona (Carolyn [Burris] Petering), Louisiana (Gerald Van Pelt), and Florida (Jay Scheiding, Richard Schwartz, Janice [Sensenbaugh] Beaver, and Betty Joan [Smith] Eckman). Her sister, Titia Rose [Smith] Holmes came down from Greenville, Ohio.

The Ohio Pure Food Company

Most people are surprised to learn that Gordon was the home of the

Ohio Pure Food Company that produced chocolates and peanut butter among other things. The Townsend family owned it. Susan Townsend, owned 4 acres of ground along North Street and at the head of East Street on a 1910 map. In the 1920s and 1930s, daughters Ella and Emma lived together in a home on Lot 9 on Perry Street. Their advertisement reads: *"Townsend's Chocolate Makes the Best Things to Eat. Layer Cake, Devil's Cake and Chocolate Pie, made of Townsend's Chocolate are good enough for queens, preachers and sweethearts. A 10-cent package of Townsend's Chocolate powder makes a pound and half of better candy than can be bought at any price and is easily and quickly made. Made only by The Ohio Pure Food Company, Gordon, Ohio."*

The Gordon Coal and Hardware Company

Charles "Buck" Eichelbarger was the clerk for this company. His bookkeeper was Ruth [Rice] Lage. This business was a lumber company that handled hardware and sold coal. The Francis and Rosser Company of Arcanum, Ohio owned it.

The Warwick Hotel

The Warwick Hotel was located on Lot 15 (1857 Gordon Plat Map). Weston Warwick was the owner and Gordon resident. In 1875 William Tice ran the hotel called it "Gordon Town Hotel."

The Jones and Flory Restaurant

John Sam Jones (Emma, and their children, Welthy G., Paul S., Edith M., Lucille A., Jeanette J., Margaret and Harry) owned the "best restaurant in town" and also a meat market on Main and Perry Streets. John S. or "Sam" Jones was a respected citizen and elected to the post of town Trustee on April 5, 1901. W. W. Pierce, Trustee Board President signed the declaration. Margaret Jones was photographed on the lawn of the Blue Ribbon Creamery. in the background is the town pump and water trough. Across the street is the "Mont" Mundhenk grocery store. The Jones' establishment also kept boarders. People lived there in rooms upstairs. Helen [Flory] Gentner and Grace [Idel] Fisher both confirmed this to me in April 1998. The business operated out of the Jones home on Main Street situated on the split Lot 13. Lot Thirteen was subdivided before 1857 and was owned in 1857 by Weston Warwick. The building was beside the former John Layton general store that was then being operated by "Mont" Mundhenk. Grace [Idel] Fisher told me (April 3, 1998) that there was a narrow gate and walk between the two buildings that led to an entrance in the Jones property. Grace said the freshly butchered meat was sold from what had been the living room. The restaurant was in operation in the large dining room in the house. The Jones family occupied the remainder of the dwelling. The building was torn down and the empty lot was used for a vegetable garden by the Boyer family who operated their grocery store next door. For tax purposes, the lot was only ten feet wide, and the store owner was obligated to pay the taxes on the ground.

Ira Flory and Esta Flory owned the other restaurant in town. Helen [Flory] Gentner's father, Ira and mother, Esta, owned the restaurant and home on the corner of North and Main Streets. Helen said her brother, Roy Flory, was only a baby when the restaurant was in business. Helen said they "mostly" sold sandwiches to workers and people in the neighborhood.

People who knew, told me that before 1900, liquor flowed like tap water in Gordon. It has been bone-dry since I was born and will probably remain that way (see Saloon).

There were other boarding houses in town that served meals and might have served beer. The J. S. Jones Restaurant kept boarders in their establishment on Main Street, and so did Ira and Esta Flory on north Main Street. Many private homes had borders living in them.

The Gordon Saloon

The first saloon appears to have been located in the old Gordon Station house located next to Ammon's store. In a photograph showing a near baby Ruth Rice feeding pigs on Perry Street, this building can be seen in the background. Some people want to confuse this with the old George Myers coal office. That building was smaller and located farther south than the station office building that became the saloon. Bryan Kitt was a saloon keeper and (see Kitt family) his wife, Hannah lived in Gordon at the time. They were both from Ireland.

There were two saloons. Marvin Miller told me on May 4, 1998 that his father told him that the saloon was on the corner of Main and Perry Street on Lot 12 (that would be the home that David Lair and Sarah Gordon built and lived in). He said it was a bawdy place where men got into fights, and his father related the story that one night one of the drunken men got into a fight with another drunk. The first one took out a knife and sliced open the other man's stomach so that his bowels began to fall out. That man promptly held them with both hands and walked to Doctor Silver's office on the corner of North and Main Streets and Doctor Silver sewed the man's wound closed. Marvin said his father also told him that the "Women's Christian Temperance Union" once set sticks of dynamite off at the saloon door and blew the doors off their hinges.

The Barber Shops

When I grew up there, Henry Myers had a barbershop on the same lot. His shop was a very small building, on the corner. This was the site where the Warwick Hotel had been located. He was the barber who cut my hair for the very first time. Beside it was a town pump and water trough for horses to drink from. That water trough and pump was in front of the Warwick Hotel. Henry's mother and father, Sarah and John, still lived in their home next door in 1910. The other shop was located on South Main south of Henry's shop, and it was operated by Leo Guy.

Leo also operated a general store on Main Street.

Joe Hoke operated a barbershop in the 1950s and 1960s out of his home where he had a shop built on the west side of his house. He barbered for many years until declining health forced him to barber two or three days each week. He was a big man, who loved to talk, and had a story to tell every time you saw him. His home and barbershop was located on Lot 1 in the Post Addition along the railroad tracks. Ida and George Myers had formerly owned the house.

The Livery Stable

Holly O'Dell's father and mother, M. O. O'Dell and Anna, (a veterinary), owned the Gordon Livery Stable on North Street. They also sold livestock feed at the site. Holly's grandmother, Haner, still lived on Perry Street (1910 Gordon Directory). Holly O'Dell, the son, owned a small gasoline station on the same lot in the 1930s and 1940s. (We called him "Hol"). Hol (slang, but sounded like 'hall") cussed in every sentence. His wife, Ethel O'Dell deplored this, but it never changed. People thought that he did not even realize his vocabulary included more cuss words than anything else. His wife's name was "Ethel." Ethel had the ability to cure burn victims by speaking words over them.

Hol was a welder and was heating something on the under side of an old car with a torch used in welding. Bud Flory and I were seated on chairs (used for "loafing") watching and drinking a coke, and eating a penny's worth of peanuts. Bud Flory began nosing around and Hol lowered the burning torch to his side while he was looking up at the red-hot metal. The flame hit Bud's arm and hand. Bud screamed, and Hol called his wife, Ethel.

Ethel O'Dell Cured Burns with Words

Ethel came running and I recall that she asked Bud if he believed that she could take the burn away. Between gasps, he said, "yes," and she led the screaming Bud outside the small station. A few minutes later, when she returned, the burn was gone and Bud had stopped screaming and crying. Hol had made me stay inside and he refused to say what she did but he told me, years later, that Ethel was given this healing gift by her mother and that it could only be passed on from mother to daughter.

The Blue Ribbon Creamery

The Blue Ribbon Creamery was located in Gordon and another creamery was also located in town. The Blue Ribbon Creamery was located on Main Street, on a small triangular piece of ground just south of Lot 27.

Edna [Schaar] Snyder ran the creamery in 1927, but confessed she spent more time chasing her boyfriend around and lost the job the following year. I have a photograph of the creamery that was taken in 1927 and shows Helen [Flory] Gentner and Hannah [Reed] Cross seated on the bench in front of the building. The second town pump and watering trough are also shown in one of these photographs.

The building was the coal office of George Myers (and his wife, Ida May) when I grew up.

My half-sister (Norma Ballengee) had two of her four children (Lulu Ann and Gordon Lee - Gordon Lee Goins was killed in Vietnam) while living in this small building during WWII.

There was another creamery in town. This one was in the front of the house on Lot 20 facing Main Street. The home was then owned by Mabel

Woodbury and Lymon Woodbury who bought cream.

The General Stores

In 1857 John Layton sold boots and shoes and general merchandise from the building on Lot 13. There were several owners of this dry goods and general merchandise store in town. D. Fryman owned it in 1875, and Leo Guy, probably in 1888. Charles F. "Mont" Mundhenk and his wife Katie, owned and operated a general store and the post office on Lot 13.

In 1936, Tom Stonerock owned the same grocery store on Main Street that was previously owned by Mont Mundhenk and William Boyer. William and Lillian Boyer owned the store in the 1930s and 1940s. The post office was no longer at the site when Boyer owned the store. I was impressed at the big barrels of nails, and the big boxes of cookies setting on the oiled floor.

Boyer's grocery store carried everything from new coveralls to groceries and took fresh eggs and meat in trade. They sold anything the people in town and the country needed. Boyer also had a Reo truck, with hard tires, that John Long drove out into the country, visiting local farmers. The store sold gasoline from hand pumped pumps located next to hitching posts along the sidewalk, near the curb.

John Long sold anything the local farmers needed right off the truck and he took eggs and freshly dressed chickens in trade from cash-poor farm families.

Vern Armitage owned the store and I assume he had purchased it from Boyer. He operated the store in the 1950s and early 1960s. The store closed after Vern quite the business. The building is still there. There was another store of some significance on Main Street. It was owned in my time by Charles "Sandy" Marcum. He had been a clerk at the Levi Ammon store for seventeen years before building and opening his grocery store on Main Street in 1918. In 1998 the front of the store was remodeled and the old siding was removed. At the top were the words, "Sandys Cash Store."

The Post Office was not in the store when Sandy owned it. At that time it was still in the home of Lymon and Mabel Woodbury directly across Main Street. Their daughter, Helen, married Bob Klink.

When Sandy died on October 2, 1936 he was 62 years of age. His widow, Martha (Pace) Marcum, two sisters, Mrs. Ella (Marcum) Rice (Tommy Rice's wife - Tommy was the blacksmith) and Mrs. Lydia (Marcum) Needham of Cincinnati tried to keep the store operating but sold it. Frank Pinkerton and Opal Pinkerton eventually owned the store and the post office was in the store when the Pinkerton's owned it.

Clarence Beaver and Cary Beaver owned the store and ran the post office for a number of years, and sold the store to Everett and Helen Gentner. Everett Gentner and Helen Gentner owned this store and operated the post office there until they sold it to Carl Morris and Earlene Morris. Carl Morris ran the grocery store and post office for many years. It was the store that everyone went to pick up their mail. Stephen Bernstein and Martha Bernstein bought the grocery store from Carl and Earlene Morris.

The Town Hall

The building that we know as "The Town Hall" was originally built as a new Methodist Church after that group and the local Baptist Church members had a "falling-out." Lot 4 was purchased from Andrew Klinger for $30 and a building project was started. Members erected a frame church and dedicated it in 1861. They spent a total of $1,000.

When I grew up in Gordon, the building was used as a town hall and it was a place for townspeople to go to vote. It was also used throughout the 1940s for "Medicine Shows." The people who put on the shows lived in very small house trailers parked on the east side of East Street where two vacant Lots (47 and 48) used to be during the Second World War.

Adults attended every night there was a performance. I think admission was free and the place was packed with kids and parents. Sometimes parents bought the medicine but more often than not, no medicine would be sold, or very few bottles of it were sold. Of course, they also sold snacks to adults and kids alike. When it was cold, in the winter, someone had to keep the stoves going.

The entertainment was slap stick — at times bordering on vulgar but with a good sense of humor. The shows were always very patriotic because of the war. I remember people left feeling better than when they got there. So, in that respect, the town hall was good for the people of Gordon during the war years. Now that I come to think of it, those were lonesome years for a lot of people, especially for the parents, wives and sweethearts of those serving in the Armed Forces.

The History of the Gordon, Ohio Post Office

The first post office was established in Gordon, Ohio on February 10, 1853. The mail was sorted and put into mailboxes at Gordon Station beside the railroad tracks. The original Post Office is shown at this location in 1875 on a map. The name, Jim Longenecker, is mentioned as a postmaster in Gordon who worked out of the Gordon Station building.

From there, the post office moved across to Perry Street into the home of the Townsend sisters, Ella Townsend and Emma Townsend (Lot 9).

The Townsend girls never married, but Emma had a son, Merle Townsend, who, according to Grace [Idel] Fisher, was a nice young man -- very polite and courteous. The post office was situated in a small room on the west side of the house that was reached by a sidewalk. The Townsend family had owned and operated "The Ohio Pure Food Company" and among other things, produced "Townsend Chocolate" and "Townend Peanut Butter."

The post office moved across the street into a building that was also a general store that John Layton, Charles "Mont" Mundhenk, William Boyer and Vern Armitage would own. It is shown at this location on several maps. Katie Mundhenk was the postmaster.

Some time passed before the post office moved across Main Street, into the home of Lymon and Mabel Woodbury (Lot 26). They had a daughter, Helen. Helen later married Bob Klink and was killed in a car accident at the intersection of S. R. 722 and Gordon-Landis Road. The Woodbury family moved in with my mother and I (Vivia Lincoln on Railroad Street) for a short period of time (late 1930s or early 1940s).

Eva [Fetters] Ditmer, (Lot 26), operated the post office after her husband, William "Bill," Ditmer died and was buried at Ithaca Cemetery. After his death, Eva met William "Bill" Burris (Ralph "Waxy" Burris' father) and married him. After their marriage, the couple moved out of town to the Burris farm on the east side of Gordon-Landis Road.

The post office moved north on Main Street to Lot 18. Lymon and Mabel Woodbury once again ran the post office at this location. The Stump family owned it next and sold it to Joe and F. Arlene . Mrs. Mills still lives in the house today. From there, the post office moved directly across the street into the grocery store.

Frank and Opal Pinkerton owned the grocery store and was the postmaster for a number of years.

Clarence and Cary Beaver owned the store and ran the post office for a number of years.

A man by the name of "Furman" operated the store and post office for a few years. They had a granddaughter whose name was "Dee Dee Sheets."

Another family owned the store and ran the post office, and lived with the Idel family. They had a granddaughter who lived with them. Nobody could remember their name, not even Grace [Idel] Fisher in whose parent's house, the couple lived.

Everett Gentner owned the store and was the postmaster in Gordon for a number of years. His wife, Helen, was a postal clerk and served the post office in town for a number of years after it was moved out of the store.

Carl Morris owned the grocery store and was the postmaster. His wife Earlene and employees, Helen [Flory] Gentner and Delores [Flory] Bruner and all of the Morris' children helped in the store. During most of the period the post office was here, it was in the back corner of the store (southwest corner).

Harold Rhodehamel built the post office addition on the south side of the main building and the post office was removed there.

Stephen and Martha Bernstein bought the grocery store from Carl and Earlene Morris. The Bernstein family still lives in Gordon on Lot 12 and owns the property and Lot 11.

Jerry Thacker was a postmaster in Gordon, Ohio for several years.

After the Gordon, Ohio Post Office closed, the Arcanum Post Office (45304 Zip Code) began delivering mail to Gordon residents who were required to put up rural mail boxes in the 1990s.

The Gordon Zip Code remains 45329, although some people are now using the Zip Code for Arcanum (45304) on their mail to Gordon residents.

The Gordon Lumber Yards and Saw Mills

Ezra Post owned a lumber yard in Gordon and owned the farm west of town. The Bishop brothers operated a steam powered saw mill on the west side of the Cincinnati and Miami Railroad line next to the Tile Works. Gordon was famous for good stands of timber that was valued by the early settlers. In the vicinity were large stands of hickory and this wood was used for barrel hoops. Mary Clark's husband, Charles, moved to Gordon because he was a maker of barrel hoops and worked in one of the town's first industries a "cooperage," around 1866.

Francis and Rosser operated a lumberyard at the end of Railroad Street in 1910. Ezra Ammon owned a mill lot next to a grain elevator in 1910.

The Dohner-Mote Company owned a lumberyard, coal and cement yard on Main Street.

W. H. Ditmer was the manager of the Dohner-Mote Lumber Company. He lived on Perry Street with his wife Eva. Philip Dohner and his wife, Ella, were co-owners with Mr. Mote, of the Dohner-Mote Lumber

Company. In the 1930s and 1940s, Charles "Buck" Eichelbarger managed the same type of business on Main Street in the same building, and sold coal. The coal lay along the east side of the railroad tracks behind West Street (behind Foland 1998). Ruth [Rice] Lage was the secretary and bookkeeper. The Rosser Lumber Company from Arcanum, Ohio then owned it. George Myers sold coal and his coal yard was at the end of Centre Street next to the railroad tracks. Walk over there, face west and then look north along the tracks and that was his coal yard. Cement bins were there for many years and foundations might still be there. Bricks were sold at lumberyards for a long time.

At one time there was a Tile Works and Brickyard next to Bishop Brothers steam powered saw mill. The steam powered saw mill was south of the Ammon home (Whiting home 1998) between it and Scott Street where Roney Dean Miller lives (1998). This was immediately opposite the railroad tracks on the west side, north of the Ammon home (Whiting home 1998) and the foundation was visible in the 1940s. As children, in the 1940s, we used the foundation as forts to play "war games."

The Blacksmiths

W. H. Rice was a blacksmith in Charles' shop on Main Street. William D. Rice, the father for the boys, whose wife was Ethel, was a mechanic in his shop on Main and Perry Street. Charles Rice operated a blacksmith shop on Main and Perry Street on the lot where the Weston Warwick Hotel had been. The building had been moved to West Street when I grew up in Gordon. Tommy pounding on an anvil was my signal to get up out of bed. I shall never forget that sound. I always knew him as "Tommy" Rice. Tommy and his wife, Ella, were the parents of Ruth [Rice] Lage.

Ruth's husband, William "Bill" Lage owned a Reo auto dealership in town and sold cars and serviced them for many years. Bill was considered a good car and truck mechanic. (Jack Foland property 1998).

My father later bought the blacksmith building and moved it across the railroad to Lot 4 on Railroad Street. Bob Klink converted the old blacksmith shop into a home. (This house was the first home my wife and I owned in Gordon, Ohio.).

Ernest Rice and his wife Mary had a shop on West Street. They had a son, Leonard G. Rice.

The Doctors

Charles Overholser, a physician, had a home and office on Lot 21 in Gordon. His wife's name was Nora. They had two sons, Sanford and Jerold and one daughter, Elizabeth.

Horatio Z. Silver (wife Louisa "Lora") was a physician who lived on Perry Street. They had one daughter, Helen. Silver's office was also on Main Street where Dr. Van Pelt eventually lived and later on West Street.

Dr. George F. Van Pelt wife's name was Ella. They had a son, Gerald F. Van Pelt. Dr. Van Pelt's practice was on the corner of Main and North Street and at that time it was the finest house in town. Dr. Van Pelt was my doctor when I was born in 1934.

The Pure Oil Company

The Pure Oil Company had gasoline storage tanks and fuel oil tanks at their site at the end of Railroad Street. They also had an old barn that was used as a warehouse. Ora Hickman was the driver and Charles Myers (George and Ida's son) was the salesman.

The Grain Elevators and Grain Dealers

Levi Ammon and Sons owned the Elevator beside the railroad tracks south of Perry Street on the west side of the railroad tracks, in 1857. Ammon was a grain dealer and also operated a store from the same building.

D. S. Albright and J. Harndon had a warehouse along the railroad tracks on Lot 27 in an 1857 map of Gordon. They were grain dealers. Their building was located next to the railroad tracks on what was West Street but not yet developed. An 1875 maps shows the warehouse and store as separate buildings on the same site owned by Levi Ammon. F. M. Warwick was operating a business in 1875 beside the railroad tracks where the Albright and Harndon warehouse had been eighteen years earlier. Ed Ammon owned a grocery store where Charles "Sandy" Marcum clerked for seventeen years before he built his store on Lot 24 in Gordon. Some of Levi Ammon warehouse foundation was still along the tracks when I was a boy in the early 1940s.

The Gordon Tile Works and Steam Powered Saw Mill

In 1888 and before, the Gordon Tile Works was in production. Most of the area farms used tile that was made at this factory. The Tile Works is shown on an 1888 map as being in the southeast corner of the Ezra Post farm. This would put it directly opposite of Scott Street on the West End of that street. It was located in a field and connected to the Bishop Brothers Steam Powered Sawmill.

What Some Families Did

There were carpenters, joiners, wagon makers, harness makers, and coopers who were all busily engaged in their respective trades. John A. Grau (also spelled 'Graw') was a wagon maker living in Gordon with his wife, Rosan. His home and shop were located on Perry Street next to the alley that is there today Lot 8 in 1857.

David Lair was a harness maker and lived on Main Street and Perry on Lot 12 in 1857. His widow, Sarah [Gordon] Lair was still living in the home in 1910. His home would end up becoming a saloon in Gordon with some wild fights and dynamite bombings.

Dulcena Gordon was a housekeeper and lived on Main Street in 1910. She was called, "Cena" by the townspeople and lived in the two-story home on Lot 30 across from the beautiful home of Ed Ammon.

Charles W. Holt was a carpenter and joiner, in 1857, and lived on Perry Street (Lot 49) and his shop was on East Street (Lot 43) where the Methodist Church is located today.

In 1875, Ezra Post, who was a teacher and Notary Public, lived on Lot 22 in 1875. The wagon shop of F. Blum was located on Lot 23 in 1875. His business is listed as a "Wagon Shed."

George Post operated an insurance business on Perry Street. Mary Post and Ezra, the director of the lumber company lived on Perry Street on Lot 9.

A number of people working in the "car barn" in town, but this is a mystery. I assume it had something to do with the electric traction line, but found nobody who knew where it was located. Herman Hall and his wife, Elizabeth, lived on Perry Street. He was a plasterer.

In 1875, Mary C. Gebelein lived on Lot 9 on Perry Street. Her husband, Karl, was a wagon maker and his business is shown on the map. He is buried in Gordon Cemetery. The name was also spelled "Carl Gabelein."

The Baptist Church is located on Lot 35 in front of the Gordon Cemetery in 1875. The building is situated on the south side of the lot in the east corner.

Bryan Kitt was running the Gordon Saloon on Lot 12 in 1875. The Women's Christian Temperance Union would blow the doors off with dynamite. This had been the home of David Lair and he ran a harness shop here in 1857.

Religion in Gordon

Philip Gordon and his family built a log church on their property. At the same time, they set aside an area for a family cemetery. The family were Baptist and the first church in Gordon was this Baptist Church. Many of Philip and Elizabeth's descendants were baptized in this log church. There is a 1911-newspaper clipping that describes the death of Andrew Gordon's widow, Sarah Ann Gordon. The funeral services were held at the Gordon Baptist Church, Monday, March 6, 1911 at ten o'clock. Services by Frederick Fischer of Greenville. She was buried beside her husband at Ithaca Cemetery.

About the year 1830, a few Methodist Families met for worship in the home of Alanson Ashley and Jane Ashley (where Milbert Ressler and Bonnie Ressler lived – in 1985 it was the Ed Boomershine farm just north of the Preble County Line Road) on present Gordon-Landis Road. In 1835, Edmund C. Thomas bought the Ashley Farm and in that year the society was organized and Edmund Thomas was appointed the first class leader. Reverend Charles Swain was the circuit preacher who organized the work and the "Thomas Class" was listed as a regular appointment on the Eaton circuit. George H. Post settled in Gordon and with the Thomas Class membership at 41 in 1843, the society launched a building project.

On July 11, 1843, John K. Owen sold 30 square rods of what is now the Lynch farm (1985 the Eugene Lambert place) for $10. The society erected a log church and it was recorded on the Lewisburg circuit as the "Thomas Meeting House." An old account describes the backless slab seats supported by four pins and the tallow candles that required a snuffer to extinguish. There was a large iron stove in the center and for the next 14 years the log church served its noble purpose. Rapid decay and an enlarging congregation forced the members to favor a new location in town. In 1857 the log church was abandoned and the members focused attention on and joined forced with the Baptist society in town located near the Gordon family cemetery (see abandoned cemetery).

The Baptist Church was repaired and the Methodists transferred their slab seats to the Baptist Church. For a time everything went along well until, it is reported, that some in the Baptist Church developed an intolerant attitude toward the Methodists and that resulted in the Methodists withdrawing altogether.

For a period of three years the Methodists met various places including a room upstairs at the Stonerock Grocery Store. In 1857, the trustees had purchased Lot 4 from Andrew Klinger for $30 and the faithful members now erected the frame church used today as the Town Hall. The quarterly conference of August 3, 1861 reported that the house was completed except for the pulpit and seating arrangements and still needing $100 to clear the enterprise of all debt. It was dedicated later that year having cost $1000. It was 46 x 36 feet. All of the seats used in the church were constructed from one walnut tree that was cut down on the Levi Thomas place north and east of town. Some authority has estimated that the tree would have been 40 inches in diameter at the cut off and able to make a log 24 feet long.

The congregation continued to grow and in 1877 when Gordon became the head of a new circuit and in 1882 a parsonage was moved on the church lot. In 1883 an addition was made at the north end of the church and a new bell provided all being paid for out of a $1000 bequest to the church by William Graham. The church continued to grow and on February 16, 1901, Andrew McClain sold to Ezra Post, and trustees, Lots 43 and 44 for the sum of $200 with a stipulation that a church building must be built in one year. On November 28, 1901 a new church was ready for dedication. The Baptist Church fell into ruin and the congregation had to attend services elsewhere. The Methodist Congregation is still intact in town and membership has not varied much over the years.

Sources:

Whenever possible I sent personal letters and forms to relatives of people who I knew once lived in Gordon, Ohio. A lot of information was obtained in this fashion for more recent residents. The older and original residents came from census reports, cemetery inscriptions, Bible entries, and county and township and business directories. Data came from various sources, including personal family records, interviews, and from published newspaper accounts. Names and lot numbers from 1949, 1957, 1875, 1888, and 1910 maps. Information was also obtained from Gordon Directories, especially the 1910 and 1949 directories, and from census records from 1820, 1830, 1850, 1860, 1870, 1880, 1900, 1910 and 1920. Census records are suitable for residents of Twin Township but Gordon was not platted until 1849, so the only relevant census for this work begins with the 1850 census. Helen [Flory] Gentner and Grace [Idel] Fisher were very helpful in providing information about residents, businesses and some dates.

Contact Information

The simple way is Email at popslinc@yahoo.com. You can write to Abraham at: Abraham Lincoln, Brookville, OH 45309.

About the Researcher

Abraham Lincoln was born on October 25, 1934 just as the clock was striking twelve o'clock, the son of Lurton Clarence Lincoln and Vivia Elizabeth [Ballengee] Lincoln. Emma Shoenfelt assisted in the delivery as midwife.

Abraham married Patricia Ann [Custer] Lincoln from Arcanum, daughter of Harold and Olive May Custer on July 12, 1955 in Richmond, Indiana. They have five children. Angela Beth, Christopher Patrick Lincoln, Melinda Annette, Rebecca Sue, and Melissa May.

Pat is a 4th cousin, 4 times removed to General George Armstrong Custer of Little Big Horn fame.

Abraham is President Abraham Lincoln's 3rd cousin 3 times removed.

Abraham has a Website, presently located at the following address. On this site can be seen more information about the people from Gordon, Ohio. Abe's World Wide Web address is: www.oldmanlincoln.com.

The Families

The Adams Family

Berlyn and Lilly Adams lived in Gordon on Railroad Street on Lot 4 in the 1960s. The family moved to southern Ohio and Berlyn is deceased.

The Albright Family

The earliest map of Gordon shows three lots belonging to the Albright Brothers. One is owned by A. Albright (Adam) and is Lot 2 on East Street. The other two lots are also on East Street and are Lots 48 and 42. In 1857, D. S. Albright (Simpson) and Harndon owned a warehouse and dealt in grain. This warehouse was on the east side of the railroad tracks beside Lot 27. Levi Ammon and sons would eventually buy the business and operate it. In 1910, Ruth Albright lived on East Street and is listed in the directory as a housekeeper. Glendela Albright, daughter of P. H. & C. died February 6, 1867 - age 6 months 6 days and is buried at Gordon Cemetery. Allen Albright, 1830-1899 - Elizabeth (Wife) 1828-1887are buried side by side at Gordon Cemetery. Allen served in the Grand Army of the Republic. Susan [McLaine] Albright, daughter of Isaac & Mary died October 10, 1852 - age 1-9-17 and is buried at Gordon Cemetery.

The Ammon Family

Levi Ammon and Sons owned the general store on south Main Street. Edward Ammon was a grain dealer and a merchant. His store was on Lot 27 along the railroad tracks. His wife's name was Amanda. They had two sons, Earl and Leroy "Roy". Leroy Ammon was a clerk in Ed Ammon's store on South Main. Earl Ammon was a grain merchant whose warehouse was also situated along the railroad tracks. Earl's wife's name was Estella. Levi Ammon is shown as the owner and operator of a warehouse and store on the west side of the railroad tracks on an 1888 map of Gordon. He also owned 2 acre of land next to Rebecca Troutman. In addition, in 1888, he owned 4.53 acres of ground south of the Baptist church and cemetery in the south end of Gordon.

The Anderson Family

John D. Anderson died May 30 1869 - age 77 years 9 months. His wife, Maggie, died August 26, 1895 when she was 73 years of age. James Anderson, died March 25, 1868 - age 77 years 9 months. All are buried at Gordon Cemetery.

The Armitage Family

Vern Armitage and his wife, Merle, owned the General Store on South Main Street on Lot 13 in Gordon in the late 1940s and 1950s until it closed and was bought by Joe Hoke. John Layton, Charles F. "Mont" Mundhenk, and Bill Boyer formerly owned it. Vern loved to go fishing and he would often leave the store on Wednesdays to drive to Ithaca to go fishing in the creek there.

The Ary Family

I remember Ralph and his wife, Olive, and their children, Roberta, Gene and Richard "Dick" Ary. They lived on the old Sarah Condon property along North Street beside the railroad. The lot was a triangular piece of land of about 1 acre opposite or west of Lot 7 in Brown's Addition. They always had a pony or horse and Ralph, the father, was always making wagons for the family to use. He was quite a wagon maker. Ralph also put the first rubber tires on a steam engine that I ever saw. He cut off the cleats and welded a tire rim on and added rubber tractor tires. He operated out of "Ary's Welding Shop" beside the house on North Street.

He made the first "Buck Rake" I saw and those were used by farmers to take in hay. The Buck Rake was an old Model T or a Model A Ford that he cut the back and welded a beam and winch and attached a crank and cable on the frame. On the beam were pointed tobacco rails. They stuck out like the tines of a fork. The operator got in the cab and backed the contraption down a row of hay. The hay collected on the forks and when the operator could no longer see where to back up, the load was cranked-up at an angle and driven into the barn. Ralph Waldo Ary died and was buried at age 65 on February 25, 1970. He is buried at Ithaca Cemetery.

The Bader Family

Philip Bader was a carpenter. His wife was named Jessie J. He lived on south Main Street. Jessie was a music teacher. They had three sons, Rollis, Philip Jr., and Ernest C. They had one daughter Ethel I. Philip Jr. married Bernice and lived on Main Street on Lot 22 until his death. He was buried at age 66 on August 3, 1960 at Ithaca Cemetery. Bernice came to Gordon in 1918 and has lived there since. Philip Jr. and Bernice had one son, Marvin Bader who presently lives in Louisville, Kentucky. Philip was a truck driver, driving for D. G. U. Trucking Company. In 1910, Philip Bader owned 3.5 acres of land east of East Street but within the corporation limits of Gordon. Ota Bruner lived with Philip and Bernice until her death.

The Baker Family

Dewey Baker and his wife Grace lived on Main Street on Lot 15. Leonard D. Baker and his wife, Grace, lived on Main Street. He was an assembler at Frigidaire, Division of G. M. C. in Dayton. Lowell B. Baker and his wife, Billy, lived on Main Street. They had two children, Billy and Johnie. He was a trucker.

The Ballengee Family

Vivia Elizabeth May Ballengee, was born, in 1909, on a small farm in the mountains around Hinton, West Virginia. Her mother died on November 4, 1922 after giving birth to Elsie May, the youngest daughter. Vivia, the oldest at thirteen years of age, had to quit school and take care of the needs of the family. Her father, James or "Jim" Ballengee had married Elsie May Richmond and the marriage produced Vivia, William Evert, Lossie Franklin, Hazel, Minor David, Ethel Lorain, Violet Pauline and Elsie May. Jim Ballengee was jailed for making moonshine and mother recalls that people used to come to their cabin to buy it by the quarts. Vivia had one daughter, Norma Ruth Ballengee while in West Virginia. Vivia and Norma moved to Ohio when Norma was a small child. Norma Ruth [Ballengee] Goins lived on Railroad Street on Lot 5 in the Post Addition in the late 1930s and early 1940s. She was the daughter of Vivia Elizabeth [Ballengee] Lincoln who lived there with her husband, Lurton Clarence Lincoln and son, Abraham Wesley Lincoln. She went to Gordon School and graduated from Verona High School. She married Roy Lee Goins from West Sonora and had Lulu Ann, Gordon Lee (killed in Vietnam), Ruth Elaine and Roy Goins Junior.

The Barklow Family

Hendrick Barklow was born September 25, 1816 and died May 31, 1895. He was 78 years old. His wife, Elizabeth was born January 3, 1819 and died December 23, 1903. She was 89. Alma Barklow was born in Franklin, Tennessee, the daughter of Theodore and Ida Eller. Alma married Russell Barklow and they had six children. One of the children is Alice [Barklow] Dickey who lives in Arcanum. Alma lived her entire life on a farm near Gordon, Ohio. Russell Barklow was born in 1888 and is buried at Ithaca Cemetery. Alma-died and was buried on December 26, 1994 at age 104 at Ithaca Cemetery. Another daughter, Marjorie born March 18, 1922 died December 22, 1924. Samuel Barklow and his wife, Ellenora "Ellen" listed in Gordon with their son, Orien B. Samuel was born July 25, 1851 and died January 4, 1920. His wife, Ellenora was born February 22, 1852 and died December 30, 1945. Laura was born

September 25, 1816 and died May 31, 1895 aged 78. Samuel born July 25, 1851 died January 4, 1920. Elizabeth born January 3, 1814, died December 23, 1903. Buried at Gordon Cemetery.

The Barnhart Family

Charles Barnhart was an "oiler." His wife was named Lena. She was a "tobacco sizer." They had daughters, Relva M., Grace M., and Alice M., and sons, Emil L. a laborer, Lawrence E. a laborer, Harry R., Virgil T., Charles L., and Loyd E. They lived in Gordon in 1910.

The Bechtol Family

Sarah Bechtol, wife of Daniel Bechtol, born May 10, 1836 died November 12, 1880. Mary E. Bechtol daughter of Daniel & Sarah died October 7, 1874 - age 11-9-19. Daniel died May 24, 1896 - age 63-1-14, and this family are buried at Gordon Cemetery. William Bechtol's wife was Idella "Della" Myrtle [Troxell] Bechtol. Their children were Bonnie Marie (Harold Dwight Ressler's mother), Owen Salvanis "Butch", and Mamie O. Bechtol. William Bechtol had two brothers, David and Charley and one sister, Martha D. Bechtol (Charles Rauscher's grandmother). Owen Salvanis "Butch" Bechtol, born October 17, 1898 was Bonnie [Bechtol] Ressler's brother. Butch and his wife, Maudie Blanche "Bobbie," born May 11, 1904, lived on a farm that adjoined the Gordon School property. They lived on the farm in the 1930s, 40s, 50, and early 1960s. They had two sons, William "Bill" and Larry. Bill died in 1998 and is buried in Texas. Bill was born November 26, 1931. He married Millie Isaacs from Verona. They moved to San Marcos, Texas and have three children. Pepper is a principal in San Antonio, Susan is married to a granite salesman and teaches in Marble Falls, and Bob works in warehousing at the University of Texas. Larry was born October 14, 1937 at Gordon. He married Betty Jean [Jacoby] Bechtol. She was born January 11, 1936. His children are Julie Lynn Riedy, born August 14, 1958, and Lori Ann Patton born November 30, 1962. Stephen Bret Bechtol was born December 10, 1963 and Joan Elizabeth Bechtol was born September 2, 1965. Melissa Dawn Geiger was born November 12, 1967 and Adam Sean Bechtol was born June 14, 1969. Tarla Marget Bechtol was born August 25, 1971. Larry became an ordained minister in the United Church of Christ. He had Bret, Joan, Sean and Tarla and was divorced from his first wife. In 1986 he married Beth Geiger and became a stepfather to Julie, Lori and Melissa. They live in Cincinnati, Ohio.

The Bernstein Family

Stephen Bernstein and family live in Gordon, Ohio at 401 Main Street. Stephen and Martha bought the grocery store in town that the Morris Family operated for a number of years.

The Bishop Family

The Bishop brothers owned the Steam Powered Saw Mill, beside the Gordon Tile Works (see Tile Works) in Gordon in 1857. T. L. Bishop lived on Lot 30. Facing Main Street, bordered by Scott Street on the south. Andrew Gordon would own the house buy 1875.

The Black Family

Andrew Black died April 14, 1896 - age 46-9-27 and his wife, Lanie died June 9, 1892 - age 37-4-29. Cleo B. Black died June 15, 1905 - age 1 month. Cora E. Black, daughter of Andrew and Lanie died October 7, 1892 - age 12-1-16 . Ola M. daughter of Andrew and Lanie died September 15, 1890 - age 1-3-22. Emma Jane Black, daughter of J. & C. died September 25, 18?? - age 1 month 25 days. All are buried at Gordon Cemetery. Ova O. daughter of Andrew and Lanie died July 6, 1892 - age 3 months - s/sJesse H. Black and his wife, Levina Frances Black, lived in Gordon on south Main Street. They had one daughter, Martha "Mattie." Jesse worked in the railroad powerhouse. Frances is listed as a widow in the census after 1910. She was living with Mary Clark, a widow, on East

Street. Frances Black and his wife, Ruby Black, moved to Gordon in 1951 and lived in the Dohner house on North Street in the 1950s opposite or west of Lot 1 in Post Addition. The had a son and daughter, James and Marilyn Black. James got married in 1969 and lives two miles outside of Gordon on Gordon - Landis Road. Marilyn [Black] Robinson married Paul Robinson in 1963. They have two sons, Kevin and Douglas. The family is divorced and Marilyn lives on West Street in Gordon. Laura Black lived in the south end of town in 1910. She was listed as a domestic in the census of that year.

The Bliss Family

Frank Bliss and his wife, Ceville are listed as residents of Gordon, Ohio on Lot 15 in the 1936 Directory of Darke County, Ohio - Directory of Gordon, page 60. Her name is spelled Civilla in the 1920 Darke County, Ohio census, and page 363. They had Ed Bliss and Eva Bliss. Eva Bliss married Otwin Fourman. Frank began his residency in town when he is shown, in the Darke County, Ohio Census for 1880, living with Henry and Catharine Foreman as a border.

The Blose Family

Emmer T. Blose, 1881-1922, (28 in 1910) and his wife Hattie [Harleman] Blose, 1886-1952, (24 in 1910) had a daughter, Madonna. He was a carpenter by trade and built the home on North Street on Lot 4 where Ralph Fisher lived with I was a boy. William Blose lived on West Street and was a retired farmer. His wife, Charity, lived with him. Catharine E. Blose was a widow who lived on Perry Street. She was listed as 73 in 1910.

The Blum Family

F. Blum lived on Lot 23 in Gordon in 1875 and had a wagon shed on his property.

The Bolinger Family

Henry A. Bolinger and his wife, Tina R. lived in Gordon with their daughter, Mary E. Bolinger. He was a ticket agent at Gordon Station (or an agent for the railroad). Horatio S. Bolinger died September 2, 1893 at age 25 and is buried at Gordon Cemetery. Lette M. Bolinger died April 14, 1891 age 20. An infant born April 7, 1891 is buried beside the mother. Lawrence Bolinger born February 22, 1909 died July 26, 1909. M. Bolinger was the father of Lawrence. M. Bolinger was born in 1817 and died August 28, 1900, age 83. Annie G. Bolinger, his wife, died August 6, 1890. She was born in 1824. They are all buried at Gordon Cemetery.

The Bonham Family

Uriah S. Bonham lived on Lot 28. He was 58 in the 1880 Darke County, Ohio Census and his wife Susan had died November 15, 1866. She was 31. . His children, Ann, Amanda, Dulcina and Andrew were living with him as was his brother, Amos. His children Sarah died July 6, 1860 age 3 months and Ambrose died August 25, 1862, age 5 months. Uriah S. Bonham died February 11, 1886 age 64. Uriah Bonham and his wife, Elisabeth lived on Lot 28 in 1875. He was a shoemaker from New Jersey. He was 32 in the 1880 Darke County, Ohio Census and his wife was 30. Amos Bonham died January 25, 1893, age 74 and he is buried in Gordon Cemetery with the rest of the Bonhams who lived in Gordon.

The Boyer Family

William and Lillian Boyer lived in Gordon and owned the Boyer Grocery Store on South Main Street. This is the oldest store in town (still standing in 1998). The Ammon store (possibly older) burned along with the Gordon Coal and Hardware Store that was the home of Bobby and Alice Harleman. The Boyer's grandson, Richard "Dick" Boyer left town in 1948 and moved to Verona with his father. Dick Boyer graduated from Verona in 1954 and presently lives in Frankfort, Kentucky with his wife and three daughters and three grandchildren. Bill Boyer bought the store from Tom Stonerock who ran it through at least 1936 since he is listed as the owner in a 1936 Directory of Darke County, Twin Township, Gordon, Ohio (Lot 13). Boyer's Store was a wonderful place for a kid to visit. The candy was displayed in a glass candy case at the front of the store. Hardware of all kinds was in boxes, bins and wooden kegs on the floor and on shelves. During World War II, the candy disappeared and none was sold until about 1945. We kids bought Smith Brothers Cough Drops as a substitute. The cherry flavored was my favorite candy substitute.

The Brown Family

William "Bill" Brown born May 13, 1958 and his wife, Kathy [Arnett] Brown, born March 24, 1958, have a son, Maxwell Austin "Max" Brown. Max was born on January 31, 1991 at Grandview Hospital. The Browns have lived in Gordon since 1992. Max said, "I was only 1_ years old so it's the only home I've known. My dad is on town council and is also park commissioner. Mom and I go to church at Gordon United Methodist Church. Gordon is a great place to live." (1998)

Alvin Brown and his wife, Anna lived in Gordon, Ohio with daughters, Leafy M., and Sada M., and son, Clarence A. Brown. Alvin was a carpenter in 1900. Samuel Brown lived in Gordon with his wife, Della. They had two sons, Calvin H., and Willie E. Brown and one daughter; Altha C. Samuel was a carpenter in the 1900 Darke County, Ohio

Census.

The Bruner Family

Wilbur Bruner (Bernice [Bruner] Bader's brother) and Onda Bruner lived on East Street (Lot 46) with their son, William "Billy". Billy used to deliver newspapers in Gordon. Bill is married and has three children. They live in Dayton, Ohio.

The Bunger Family

William K. Bunger and his wife, Bessie Esther, lived on Lot 5, Post's Addition, along Railroad Street. He was a laborer at Marble Cliff Quarries.

The Burris Family

Eva married William "Bill" Burris after her first husband, William Ditmer died. After Bill died Eva became the postmaster in Gordon (Lot 26). Eva and Bill Burris moved from town into the country on Gordon - Landis Road. William "Bill" Burris died and was buried at age 88 on November 29, 1950 at Ithaca Cemetery. William D. "Bill" Burris, is Ralph Burris' father. Ralph Burris' mother was Mary Elizabeth [Idel] Burris, born November 18, 1864 and died July 26, 1929. Mary's other children were Mrs. Harry Fourman of Gordon, Mrs. Augustus McGriff of Dayton, and two brothers, David Idel of Gordon and William Idel of Verona. She had one sister, Mrs. John [Idel] Flory of Gordon, Ohio. Ralph Burris was born October 19, 1898 and died May 3, 1980. He is buried at Ithaca Cemetery. Ralph married Mary Boneda [Heckman] Burris born June 29, 1898 and died November 18, 1982. Both are buried at Ithaca Cemetery. Mary's mother was Mary Elizabeth [Shepard] Burris born March 4, 1865 and died June 9, 1927. Mary's father was Henry H. Heckman born

September 6, 1864 and died in 1946. Ralph and Mary had, Thurman Byron born December 19, 1924 and died August 19, 1992. Kenneth was born October 2, 1918. Bertha Marcella [Burris] Wright was born May 16, 1922. Carolyn Phyllis [Burris] Petering was born October 5, 1936. Sharon Eileen [Burris] Hittle was born January 23, 1939, and Judy Ann [Burris] Burns was born January 27, 1941. Kenneth E. Burris was born on October 2, 1918 and married Euligene [Henninger] on October 5, 1940. They had Keith and Karl. Keith Wayne Burris born May 15, 1942 married Sharon Lee [Sargert] on November 28, 1964. Sharon and Keith had Deborah Ann Burris born October 11, 1965 and died August 6, 1983. Jeffry Burris born September 14, 1966 died on December 5, 1966. Diane Burris was born August 6, 1968 and David Burris was born November 11, 1970. Karl Leroy Burris born October 7, 1945 married Linda Ann [Lance] Burris born September 10, 1948 on July 2, 1966. They have one child, Christopher Burris born September 2, 1970. Maracella married Orlan Wright from Lewisburg on 10 July 1940. Orlan was born March 9, 1918 and Marcella was born May 16, 1922. They have two children. Darrell E. Wright born September 1, 1941 and who now lives in Centerville and Mary Jo Wright born November 17, 1946 and who lived in Miami, Florida, died on December 28, 1997. Carolyn Phyllis Burris married Emerson Petering on November 9, 1956 and had two children before moving to Tucson, Arizona. They now have three children, a son and two daughters. Emerson was born September 30, 1935 to Clarence Petering and Viola [Hypes] Petering. He had two sisters, Mayno [Petering] Weiss and Dianna Mae [Petering] Ebeling. Randall Lee Petering born July 3, 1957. Randall married Tracy Lee [Adams} Petering on August 16, 1974. They had Amy Leigh born December 29, 1974 and Joshua Randall born February 17, 1978. Amy Leigh Petering married George Tingstrom on January 1, 1994. They were divorced in July , 1996. Joshua Randall Petering married Stacy [Moody] Petering on February 7, 1998. Randy, Tracy, Amy Leigh, Joshua and Stacy all live in Eagle River, Alaska (April 1998) Randy is retired from the Air Force after 20 years of service. Darla Kay Petering born October 2, 1958 is single and lives in Tucson, Arizona. Boneda Jo Petering born September 25, 1960 married Douglas Less Pfund on November 3, 1979. They have Matthew Douglas born August 29, 1982, Jennifer Elisha born January 16, 1986 and Michael Emerson born September 4, 1991. They live in Tucson, Arizona. Judy married Wayne Burns in August 14, 1959. They have two adopted children, Tina and Jerrod and one foster son, George. Tina was born November 13, 1968. She lives with her husband, Ted Weaver. They have one son, Thomas Allen Weaver born October 17, 1996 and another son due in June 1998. They live in Palestine, Ohio. Jerrod Wayne Burns born October 9, 1970 married Kimberly [Parks] Burns on October 9, 1994. They live in Greenville and have no children (April 1998) Foster son, George Christopher Martin Elliott born August 16, 1969 and brought into the Burns family when he was 18 years old. He married Casey Jo [Illig] on July 20, 1997. They have a son, Mason George Illig born November 7, 1996. They live in Columbus, Ohio and are students at Ohio State University. Sharon Burris had polio has a child and limped badly. Sharon [Burris] Hittle had three children, Timothy, Cynthia and Scott. Sharon and her husband are divorced.

The Cawood Family

Reford Cawood (deceased) married Esther [Zimmerman] Cawood. They lived in the south end (extension of Scott Street west) on the land once owned by Cathy Schlechty - beginning after 1910. Reford and Esther had two children, Carl and Barbara. Carl B. Cawood was a pastor in Ohio for twenty-eight years before taking a job on the staff at Manchester College, in Indiana. Barbara [Cawood] Gay became a registered nurse and had two children, both girls. Her husband is deceased. Barbara lives in Washington State.

The Chambers Family

I wasn't very old when Jack and Gertrude "Gerty" Chambers sold out (Lot 25) and moved to Zephyr Hills, Florida. Before they moved, they gave us a wicker-back sofa and we were so proud of it. Helen Gentner, now in her middle 80s, recalled the name and Gertrude's nickname "Gerty".

The Clark Family

Mary Hilliard was born in April 3, 1839 in Piqua. She was one of four children and while she was very young, was separated from the family by some unfortunate domestic experience and never saw her family afterwards, except her mother once. She was raised by her uncle, Charles Hilliard who built the first house in Piqua, Ohio. Mary was a descendant of one of the original 15 families living in Piqua. She met and married James Clark who lived in Piqua and who had originally come from Illinois. He was 78 when he died in 1907. He is buried at Ithaca Cemetery. James was a cooper and it was the large stands of hickory, walnut, and oak. Hickory was used to make barrel hoops at the local cooperage. In 1866 when Mary [Hilliard] Clark, and her husband, moved to town (Lot 3) from Dayton (Shortly after their marriage, the couple had moved to Dayton on Brown Street.) she recalled, "We moved up here from Dayton when this was still a wilderness. There was nary a ditch nor a pike. We didn't expect to stay long, but here I am (seventy years later) in the same house (in 1936)." They had three children, Maggie 11, and her sister, Capetola 7, and brother, Willie 6 months. In the 1900 Census, James Clark is listed as a "fork maker." His age is not correctly shown at 41 - he was 61. In the 1880 Census, he is listed as a laborer and is 51 - that is the correct age. He must have taken-up making forks to compensate for a dwindling income since the cooperage was no longer in operation. During the Civil War, while tending their vegetable garden, Mary recalls the day the news came that Abraham Lincoln had been assassinated. "We were in our garden when the whistles blew and bells rang as news was received of Lincoln's assassination." She said, "Mr. Clark voted both times for Lincoln (he voted in the Gordon Town Hall for ten presidential elections). My husband always was a Whig (Republican)." Mrs. Clark was the third oldest voter in the 'Old Voters' contest run by the Dayton News. The contest was won by John Lafferty, then 100. Mary Clark was the great-grandmother of Clark and John Ray Davidson. The boy's father, John Oliver Davidson, lived in Dayton. After her husband died, Mary raised the boys. Mary was 97 years and 11 months old when she died and is buried in Ithaca Cemetery. She had an attack of influenza and after 5 days passed away. She was baptized a Baptist when 11 years of age and was a member of the Gordon Baptist Church until it closed and then she worked in the Methodist Church and for many years taught a girl's class.

The Clarke Family

Sarah Ellen [Thawley] Clarke born June 2, 1900, died November 11, 1987, buried at Memorial Gardens, Mt. Healthy, Ohio, married Frank Clarke. Frank was born November 22, 1898, died April 10, 1989, buried Memorial Gardens, Mt. Healthy, Ohio. They had three children, Wesley, Dorothy and Donald Clark. Wesley Clark married Reva Laurine [Marling] Clarke and had three children. David, born February 26, 1953. David married Tracy [Anderson] Clarke. They had one child, Sara So, born October 28, 1996. They live in Ohio. Richard James Clarke is not married. He was born February 20, 1957 and lives in Ohio. Martha L. [Clarke] Balogh married Curt Balogh on January 4, 1955. They had two children, Brittnay L. born May 30, 1986 and Tara L., born October 30, 1982. They live in Texas.

The Clem Family

Melvin C. Clem and his wife Edna lived at the south end of Main Street in the Ammon home, across the street from the home where Cena Gordon lived. Melvin was an assembler at Hobart Manufacturing Company in Troy. He was also the town marshal for a number of years and carried a revolver in a holster. Esta Clark lived with the family for a period of time.

The Collins Family

Samuel Collins and his wife Rebecca A. "Anna" Collins lived in Gordon in 1900 (census). They had two sons, Harry and Dale and one daughter,

Iva Collins. Samuel Collins is listed as a "teamster." They lived on East Street.

The Cook Family

Barbary Cook, a widow at 43, from Holland, lived in Gordon in 1880. She had two daughters, Elisabeth and Catharine and three sons, John, Henry and Andrew. At the time, Lewis Guitife was living with them as a border and worked as a laborer

The Cooper Family

Margaret Cooper lived in Gordon, Ohio in 1900. She was a widow from Ireland who had arrived in 1850. See the Darke County, Ohio Census for 1900.

The Cordell Family

Alma [Griffith] Cordell lived in an apartment which was built in Joe Hoke's (the barber) garage. This was on Lot 1 in Gordon. She lived there for 17 years until declining health forced her to move to Centerville, Ohio with her son, Carl. Alma had lived in the Ezra Fourman home (Lot 1 Brown Addition) until it was sold and from there she lived in the garage apartment owned by Joe Hoke that was on Lot 7 in the Brown Addition, previously owned by Frank Rhodehamel. Joe sold that building to Delbert Hofacker and Alma moved to the garage apartment on the Hoke property on Lot 1. Alma was Esta [Griffith] Flory's sister and much loved by her neighbors who called her a saint.

The Corzatt Family

Edward G. "Ed" Corzatt lived on Main Street on Lot 20 with his wife, Louise and children Earl and Marie L. Corzatt. Ed was a laborer. Louise (Louisa?) was from Germany. Charles "Guy" Corzatt and his wife, Addie, lived on Perry Street. He was a carpenter. They had three sons, Hubert L. Bevin H. and Parn H. The family moved to Arcanum from Gordon. Charles was a carpenter. Guy was born in 1878 and died in 1938, and his wife, Addie, born in 1883, and died in 19__ (Fresh Grave when stones were being read) are buried at Gordon. Charles died and was buried on July 13, 1938 at Gordon Cemetery. Louise died and was buried at age 53 on May 19, 1928 at Ithaca Cemetery. Eliza Corzatt lived on Perry Street and was a widow. George H. Corzatt, a member of Company C. 4th Ohio Cavalry is buried at Gordon Cemetery.

The Cross Family

John and Alice Cross moved into the Poe house on Lot 32, and lived there for many years. They had one daughter, Barbara. Bill Stewart and his family lived in the same house in the late 1940s. Roy Flory and his family lived across the street.

The Crowe Family

DeWitt Crowe and his wife, Nina, had one son, DeWitt Jr. The Crowes were farmers who lived across the road and west of Nealeigh #1, or, Gordon School.

The Curtin Family

Leonard Curtin lived on Scott Street with his wife, Dorothy. They had one child, Connie.

The Custer Family

David F. Custer, born April 28, 1854, died August 24, 1930 and his wife, Polly Ann [Henry] Custer, born October 24, 1849, died February 16, 1930, lived in Gordon on Lot 40. They had Harvey Dolan Custer, born November 24, 1883, Ida Custer, Charles A. Custer born May 6, 1878, Rose E. Custer, born February 27, 1879, L. Frank Custer, born March 9, 1880, Emery Z. Custer, born January 4, 1886, George S. Custer, born April 1, 1887, and Gertrude S. Custer, born April 1, 1888. Helen [Flory] Gentner said everyone called, Polly Ann, 'Grandma Custer.' This Custer (see Lincoln) family is my wife's Great Grandparents.

The Davidson Family

Davis Oliver Davidson, born 1879, died 1958 and Mary Clark Davidson, born 1893 and died 1918, both buried at Sugar Grove Cemetery, had a son, Clark Oliver Davidson, born July 18, 1914, died September 7, 1979 (Buried at Arlington Cemetery). Clark Oliver Davidson married Martha Alice [Earnst] Davidson, born January 13, 1920, died March 10, 1986 (Buried at Arlington Cemetery) the daughter of James William Earnst, born August 28, 1880 died January 21, 1959 and Cora May [Erbaugh] Earnst, born September 14, 1893, died December 12, 1969. Their children are Mary Madonna Davidson, born July 21, 1941 and William Oliver "Bill" Davidson, born September 21, 1947. Bill married Barbara Ray in July 1967 and was divorced in 1971. He married Helen Perkins in 1973 and was divorced in 1976. He has one son, Michael Lee Davidson, born September 7, 1974. Clark and Martha and family lived on Lot 3, on East Street in Gordon, Ohio. Mrs. James Clark lived in this house and cared for Clark, Ray and Iona Davidson beginning when she was 84 years of age (see Clark Family). At that time, when Clark was 8, Ray was 7 and Iona was 6, and their mother died, Mary Clark cared for them until they were grown. Clark "Fat" Davidson worked in Dayton throughout his lifetime and served as the town marshal and mayor on a number of occasions. Martha was nearly blind when I knew her. Mary [Davidson]

Foland lives in Gordon on Main Street where Eva [Fetters] Ditmer had the post office. Bill Davidson lives in the some home on East Street.

The Diefenbaugh Family

Henry and his wife Martha Diefenbaugh lived in Gordon with their daughter, Georgie in 1880. Henry was listed as an art. (Possibly an artist or artisan).

The DeLong Family

Neil Edward DeLong, born October 5, 1940 at Columbus, Ohio, the son of Alice [Hutchins] DeLong and Robert Rufus DeLong, and his wife, Judith A. [Fella] DeLong, born in Dayton, Ohio, the daughter of Rosemary P. [Holtmann] Fella and Leo H. Fella live in Gordon, Ohio on Perry Street (1970 - to date in 1998). Alice and Robert DeLong had another son, Michael DeLong, born September 28, 1938. Neil and Judith had Kimberly, born August 7, 1961, Diana, born November 30, 1962, Todd Michael, born February 24, 1964, Douglas, born July 28, 1965, Maria A. born March 16, 1967, Suzanne, born May 1, 1970, and Julie E., born July 9, 1971. Kimberly graduated from Transylvania College at Lexington and is a Computer Analyst Programmer. Both boys served in the U. S. Army. Douglas is making it a career and is in Intelligence/Communications and has an Associates Degree from Maryland College. Maria is a graduate of Sinclair College and lives in Vandalia. Suzanne graduated from University of Dayton and received a Masters in Library Service from Kent State and is Children's Librarian in Marion, Ohio. Julie graduated from Capitol U. Columbus and has a Masters from the University of Kentucky and is now employed by Lexmark. The DeLongs also have ten grandchildren.

The Ditmer Family

William, born in 1871 died in 1923, "Bill" Ditmer's wife's name was Eva [Fetters] Ditmer, born in 1873 and died in 1953. Bill and Eva are both buried at Ithaca Cemetery. Bill was the manager of the Dohner - Mote lumberyard. The family lived on Perry Street at the time. Eva was a music teacher. They moved to Main Street and Eva became the postmaster for Gordon for a number of years after Bill died. She became interested in William "Bill" Burris and married him (See Burris).

The Dohner Family

Philip M. Dohner and his wife, Ella, lived in Gordon in a home on a Lot next to Lot 1, Post Addition along Railroad Street. Their lot was west of Lot 1 across the alley. George and Ida Myers were their neighbors. The Black family lived there after Mrs. Dohner died. Arland Dohner became a teacher. Donald Dohner is the only surviving son (in 1998) and lived in Miami County. They had Perry, Arland, Howard, Walter and Donald. Mr. Dohner, the father was a partner in the Dohner - Mote Company, in Gordon. The business is listed in a 1910 directory as handling lumber, lath, shingles, cement, plaster and coal. The company was located in what became the Rosser Lumber Company building on Lot 27. Because of pressing financial issues, Philip hung himself. The building later became the home of Bobby and Alice Harleman. Their son, Neil Harleman, recently built a new home on the same lot.

The Drew Family

Myron Drew and his wife, Mary and children Judy, James and Jerry lived on North Street. He was a Salesman for Garbig Brothers in Jaysville, Ohio.

The Eichelbarger Family

Eichelbarger was a large family. There was Mary, a widow, above, who lived with her brother, John Hanes, on North Street. Mary died and was buried at Ithaca Cemetery at age 72 on April 27, 1926. George Eichelbarger was married to Sarah E. George was also known as "Joseph." Sarah E. Eichelbarger died and was buried at Ithaca Cemetery on November 15, 1929 at age 87. Francis Eichelbarger and his wife Etta had several children. They always lived in the south end across the railroad tracks from Lots 23 and 24. Their children were: Cecil, Treva, Ivalue and Charles "Buck." When Etta and Francis passed away, Ivalue went to stay with her grandparents George and Sarah Eichelbarger. Charles "Buck" married and his wife's name was Izora. Charles was a head saw miller (1900 census). He and Izora had two sons, Rubin and William. Charles was listed as a "cement contractor" in the 1910 Gordon Directory, but took over the daily operations of the old Rosser Lumber Company (called the Gordon Hardware and Coal Company) and ran it until it was closed. Izora died and was buried at Ithaca Cemetery at age 81 on October 1, 1956. Reuben Eichelbarger was married to Maude and they had one son, Deo Eichelbarger, born January 6, 1912. Reuben Eichelbarger died at age 76 and was buried at Ithaca Cemetery on March 19, 1970. William Eichelbarger is buried at Ithaca Cemetery at age 62 on August 20, 1958.

The Eley Family

Galen B. Eley and wife, Pearl, lived on Lot 20. They had five children, but only three lived in Gordon — Glen, Carl and Phyllis. Janice and Bill lived in New Madison, Ohio. Galen was a contractor who worked for the State of Ohio and he was self-employed. He was awarded contracts to paint bridges. Glen married Elizabeth [Jones] from Kansas, and they had sons, Mark and Scott. They live in Vandalia. Carl never married but lives with his mother, Pearl, in Huber Heights, Ohio. Phyllis was born on July 15, 1941 in District Heights, Maryland. She said the family moved to Gordon when she was in the third grade in school. Her married name is

Allen, and she has one daughter, Joan Allen. Glen Eley, Byron Harleman, myself, and Gerald Fisher used to play "horse" shooting baskets in the alley behind Gerald's house. We would spend hours doing this and seemed to have a good time when we all got together.

The Eller Family

Daniel Eller, a farmer, and his wife, Fanny, (1880) had daughters, Bell, 22 in 1880, and Ellie, 12 (Note spelling is "Ella" below). They also had sons, Theodore, 18, George 17, and Grant 15. Theodore Eller lived on Main Street with his wife, Ida. He was a farmer. They had Ruth, Vernon W., Bertha E., Glenn K., Alma R., Beatrice R., Hubert S., and Eunice N. Eller. Ella Eller lived on the last western lot on North Street and is listed on a 1910 map of Gordon as the owner. Ella Eller died and was buried at Ithaca Cemetery at age 77 on June 1, 1945. George Eller lived on the west end with his wife, Sylvia. They had two children, Victor and Mildred. George was an engineer. George died and was buried at Ithaca Cemetery at age 76 on July 18, 1939. Sylvia Eller died and was buried at Ithaca Cemetery at age 83 in 1952.

The Emrick Family

George and Kate Emrick are listed as residents of Gordon, Ohio in the 1936 Directory of Darke County, Ohio - Directory of Gordon.

The Engle Family

Alfred and Sonya [Foland] Engle live on North Street in Gordon. They have a new log cabin situated in the former John Hanes woods. It was in this woods that the famous Virginia Reunion was held, and many regular family reunions and picnics. The family recently purchased the Hanes barn and some land to round out their property in town.

The Eubank Family

E. E. Eubank (also spelled Eubanks), a retired farmer and his wife, Lottie, lived in Gordon with their 18 year old daughter, Edith according to the 1920 Darke County, Ohio Census. Hezekiah Eubanks is listed as a resident of Gordon, Ohio in the 1936 Directory of Darke County, Ohio - Directory of Gordon, page 60.

The Feitshans Family

Harry Feitshans lived on Lot 27 in Gordon with his wife Alice [Studebaker] Feitshans. She was a teacher at Gordon School — see Kids From Gordon book in the 1904 Big Room photograph. Harry Feitshans' brother, Walter, married Maude [Sellers] Feitshans. Walter and Maude's children were Rufus, Maurice, Gladys [Feitshans] Goodell, Onda [Feitshans] Bruner, Myron Feitshans, Dorothy [Feitshans] Stewart, Wendell Feitshans, and Richard. Maurice and Martha Feitshans lived on Perry Street in Gordon, Ohio. Maurice is deceased and Martha is living in Lewisburg, Ohio.

The Fellers Family

Harry A. Fellers, born in 1881 and Nellie Fellers, born in 1884 lived on Main Street. He was a self-employed carpenter. Nellie Fellers died and was buried at Ithaca Cemetery at age 88 on September 28, 1972. Harry is buried at Ithaca Cemetery. Byron L. Fellers was born in 1916 and died in 1924 and is buried at Ithaca Cemetery. Merlin Fellers had married Freda Harleman and after Freda died, Merlin lived a few years and died and was buried at Ithaca Cemetery on February 21, 1996. James F. Fellers died and was buried at Ithaca Cemetery at age 90 on August 24, 1961. His parents were James and Mary Fellers. Ida Jane was his sister. William O., John T. C., Philip C., and Harvey O. were his brothers. James was nine years old when the 1880 Darke County Census was taken.

The Fenton Family

The Fenton family moved from the Brookville, Ohio area to Gordon in 1955. Chester "Bud" Fenton, was town constable and lived on East Street on Lot 2 with his wife, Edith. Their children were, Marjorie [Fenton] Perrin, Martha, Marsha, Garry, Joe and Dan Fenton. The house they lived in on Lot 2 was torn down and is no longer there. The lot is presently owned by The Knick Family who use it as a side lawn. Across the street from this lot was the Weimer home on East Street.

The Fetters Family

Jerimiah Fetters was a 27-year-old carpenter living in Gordon when the 1870 census was taken. His wife was Clara E. and they had a son, Eddie M. Fetters and a daughter, Gertrude (1900 Darke County, Ohio Census).

The Fisher Family

Ralph D. Fisher born April 14, 1898 and died December 20, 1982 and his wife, Dorothy E. [Sensenbaugh] Fisher born March 26, 1900 and died July 14, 1983 lived in Gordon on North Street on Lot 4 in Brown's Addition. They moved to town from the country. They had two sons, Samuel Doyle and Gerald. Ralph died and was buried at Ithaca Cemetery at age 84 on December 23, 1982. Gerald Fisher married and served in the U.S. Navy and is deceased. Dorothy is deceased. Florence Sensenbaugh (Dorothy's mother) lived with the Fisher family for a number of years, until she died. Ralph was a self-employed carpenter. Samuel Doyle Fisher was born June 10, 1927. He married Juanita Louise [Kress] Fisher who was born January 31, 1928. They have two children. Beth D. [Fisher] [Oburn] Van Riper was born August 14, 1951. She has two sons, Eric M. [Oburn] Van Riper born October 27, 1972 and Andrew J. "Andy" Van Riper born March 7, 1991. Randall lives in Nevada and Beth lives in Atlanta, Georgia. Beth's husbands were Vaughn Oburn, and V. J. Van Riper born August 21, 1944. Randall C. Fisher was born June 16, 1954. His wife is Melinda [Sota] Fisher who was born January 12, 1954. They have one daughter, Megan M. Fisher, born September 23, 1985.

Earl Fisher and his wife, Grace [Idel] lived in the David Lair and Sarah [Gordon] Lair property on Main and Perry Streets when they began housekeeping. They moved from there to a farm on Gordon-Landis Road just north of town. They had two children, Dwayne and Dale. Dwayne was married and had children, but is divorced. His brother, Dale, married Shirley [Fourman] Fisher from Arcanum. They had several children. They live in Arcanum.

The John Flory Family

Michael Flory was a retired 68-year-old farmer living with his wife, Hannah, when the 1880 Census was taken. They had a son, John Flory. John Flory and his wife, Louise Luisa [Idel] Flory, moved to a farm north of town on what is now Gordon Landis Road. Louise Flory died and was buried at Ithaca Cemetery on June 11, 1930 at age 76. John Flory died and was buried at Ithaca Cemetery at age 82 on February 28, 1937. John and his wife had a son, Ira, born November 1, 1882, died October 19, 1960. Ira married Esther "Esta" [Griffith] Flory, born April 14, 1883, died September 11, 1978, and they had two children, Roy and Helen.-Ira was a first cousin to Clyde and Gus McGriff. The 1880 Census shows that John Flory and Louisa, his wife, had one daughter, Clara, then 1 year old. Ira and Esta moved to town in 1920. had a restaurant in Gordon in the house on Lot 20 where Bill and Sarah Rhodehamel would live before the Eley Family moved in. When Ira and Esta lived there, their youngest child was Roy. Helen said, "Yes they had a restaurant there, long before my time." After they sold the house on Main Street, and restaurant business, Ira and Esta and Roy moved to Railroad Street and bought the house in the Post Addition, on Lot 3. Helen and Roy lived there. Ira worked as a roofer and tinner. Helen always lived with her folks even after she was married. Roy Flory's oldest daughter, Delores, always lived with Ira and Esta, her grandparents.

Roy Flory, born July 4, 1906, died on February 4, 1990. He is buried at Ithaca Cemetery. Roy married Sarah J. [Robinette] Flory on December 9, 1927. Sarah was born March 8, 1908 and died on January 15, 1994. She is buried at Woodland Cemetery in Dayton, Ohio. They lived in a home on Lot 39 in David Lair's Addition. It was a small home with two floors and a barn out back. After a number of years, the Roy and Sarah Flory family moved to Lot 12. The harness maker, David Lair and his wife, Sarah Gordon, originally owned this Lot and home. The house reminded me of a small hotel because it had a grand entry and staircase in front that led upstairs to four rooms. Roy and Sarah had Delores, June, Richard, Robert, Bonnie, Eugene, and Bill. All of the children are still living today (April 1, 1998). Roy was a Tinner at Dayton Master Electric Company in Dayton. Delores Flory was born December 12, 1928 and she married Willard Bruner on January 30, 1948. Their children are: William Edward born March 5, 1953 married Tamela [Wherly] Bruner. Scott E. Bruner, born September 21, 1957 is divorced and has no children. He lives in Lexington, South Caroline. Barbara E. [Bruner] Mock was born May 28, 1959 and married Jerry L. Mock who was born December 23,m 1956. They were married on May 4, 1985 and have a son, Robby L. Mock, born July 30, 1985 and a daughter, Stephanie E. Mock, born December 7, 1989. The family lives in Union City, Indiana. Cara M. Bruner was born September 12, 1973 and Cortney F. Bruner was born April 1, 1978. Willard died on December 19, 1996 and was buried at Ithaca Cemetery on December 23, 1996 at age 73. Richard "Bud" Flory got married and lives in Florida with his family. His wife recently died and was buried in Florida. June Flory is married to a man whose name is Focht. She has one son. Robert D. Flory married Barbara Moore from Phillipsburg. They had five children and he is retired. They live on Albright Road east of Arcanum, Ohio. Bonnie Flory married a man whose name is Brown. She lives in Huber Heights, Ohio. Eugene "Gene" Flory is married and lives on State Route 49 North, Arcanum, Ohio. Bill Flory lives in California but was moving to Texas. My mother was the midwife who delivered Eugene and Bill Flory (I was there). Helen Flory (Roy's sister) married Clarence Rogers. Clarence died of a brain tumor and was buried at Ithaca Cemetery and Helen had a young son, Allen, to raise (see the Rogers Family). Helen married Everett Gentner. Everett bought the grocery store that Sandy Marcum has originally built and ran it and the post office. Everett sold the store to Carl and Earlene Morris. Everett and Helen had two girls -- Phyllis and Joyce. Everett died and was buried at Ithaca Cemetery (see Gentner Family) and Helen has been widowed since.

The Ray Flory Family

Ray William Flory, born September 12, 1919, died January 9, 1969 and his wife, Ruby E. [Bell] Flory, born November 29, 1915, lived west of town on Gordon-Landis Road in 1944 and after the Gordon School Picture was taken that year. The children were Robert R. Flory, Edward W. Flory, James Flory, Joseph W. Flory and Rebecca A. [Flory] Ramirez. Scott Worley was from Ruby's first husband, Scott Worley who was killed in a vehicle accident. Ray's first wife died from complications after childbirth of second child. He had two children with her, Doris and Donald. Doris [Flory] Chatterton was married for twenty-two years had five sons. Doris lives in Dayton. They were not related to the other Flory family who lived in Gordon. Robert R. Flory, born July 27, 1938, died May 13, 1996 and is buried at Castine Cemetery, and his first wife,, Helen "Sally" [Conneston] Flory had Geneva L. [Flory] Stuart who had one son, Jaren C. Kilian and one daughter Angela C. Kilian. Robert and Sally also had Gregory L. Flory who had two daughters, Raga M. and Sarah. And, Robert D. Flory who had two sons, Robert and Joseph and two daughters, Kelsi and Hanna. Robert and his second wife, Harriet J. [McMillen] Flory had one step child, Dianna L. [Minnich] Blumenstock, who had two sons, Alex L. and Eric A. Blumenstock.

The Foland Family

Jackie Lee Foland Sr., born July 7, 1941, married March 30, 1961 Mary Madonna [Davidson] Foland, born July 21, 1941, and they have two sons, Jackie Lee Foland Jr., born February 3, 1962 and Donald Eugene Foland, born January 25, 1964. Mary and Jack live in Gordon in the house where Eva Ditmer (Lot 26) lived when she ran the post office. Jack L. Foland Jr. married Rhonda [Moore] Foland and they have one daughter, Calee. Donald E. Foland married Renee D. [West] Foland and they have one son, Taylor W. Foland. They live in Florida.

The Folkerth Family

Jesse A. Folkerth and his wife, Alice lived in Gordon in 1900 (census) and is listed as a lumber laborer. They had three daughters, Ruth B., Laura J., and Anna H., and two sons, Harry S. and Charley (Charley) A. Folkerth.

The Foreman Family

Henry Foreman and his wife, Catharine lived in town in 1880 and kept a border, Frank Bliss. Frank went one to marry and have a family in Gordon (see Bliss). Henry Foreman, son of Henry and Catharine, with his wife Amanda, had sons Charles age 18, Joseph L. age 16, Sylvan age 14, and Frank age 4 and daughter Elisabeth age 11.

The Foureman Family

Gerald C. Foureman lived in Gordon with his wife Sarah. They had one daughter, whose name was Judy. They also owned "Foureman's Service Station" as late as 1949 as shown in the Gordon Street Guide for that year. Gerald worked at the Piqua Machine and Manufacturing Company. They lived in the last house on North Street going west -- the Ella Eller homestead.

The Fourman Family

Charles Ezra and Bertha Fourman lived in a home on Lot 1 in the Brown's Addition on the north side of North Street. They had two sons, Otwin and Roscoe. They also had one daughter, Amanda, called "Manda." They were still living there in 1949. Roscoe married "Lizzie" Fourman. Otwin Fourman and his first wife, Eva [Bliss] Fourman lived on Perry Street in 1910. Otwin Fourman married Bessie [Myers], Fourman, the only daughter of George and Ida Myers. They had three children, twins, son and daughter, Beverly Gene and Betty Jane Fourman, and daughter Sharon Elaine Fourman. Otwin Fourman and Bessie Mae [Myers] Fourman are buried at Abbottsville, Cemetery. Betty Fourman married Charles Rauscher in 1954 (see Rauscher for children's names). They have three children and two grandchildren. Beverly Gene Fourman (born January 28, 1934) married Janet Lee [Johns] Fourman (born June 17, 1936). They had two children, Timothy E. Fourman born November 10, 1958 and Jennifer Lynn Fourman born July 15, 1962. Beverly served as the Mayor of Arcanum for a number of years. Timothy E. Fourman married Jennifer Lynn [Strausbaugh] Fourman born March 6, 1959. They had three children, Josiah Preston Fourman born June 17, 1982, Alec McGreagor Fourman born April 1, 1986, and Katelyn Nicole Fourman born July 5, 1990. Timothy and family live in Fletcher, Ohio. Jennifer Lynn [Fourman] Knick. Jennifer has a son, Josh B. Knick born April 12, 1982. Jennifer lives with her family in Arcanum with her folks. Sharon Elaine [Fourman] (born March 7, 1941) married Bob Fourman and had two sons and one daughter. One of the boys now runs "Bob Fourman Construction" after his father passed away. Sharon has remarried. Sharon [Fourman] Wirrig married Chester R. Wirrig (born November 25, 1934). Sharon and Bob Fourman's children are: Lelah M. [Fourman] Skidmore born December 13, 1961. Lelah married Jerry W. Skidmore born

February 15, 1962. They have two children, Kyle W. Skidmore born January 9, 1984 and Derrik R. Skidmore born May 31, 1987. They live near Greenville, Ohio. Barbara Lynn [Fourman] Fourman born May 20, 1963. Barbara married Robert Fourman born February 10, 1940. They have two children, Brent M. Fourman born April 6, 1988 and Brandon R. Fourman born June 25, 1996. The family lives near Arcanum, Ohio. Charles C. Fourman born June 1, 1967 married Monica L. [Fourman] Fourman born May 13, 1966. They have one child, Sydney S. Fourman born July 22, 1995. The family lives near Arcanum, Ohio.

The Garwood Family

George W. Garwood and his wife, Rozeta B., and daughter, Esta M. lived in Gordon, Ohio in 1900.

The Gebelein Family

Christine Marie Gebelein was married to Karl Gebelein. They lived on Lot 9 in Gordon in 1875. Christine was born March 26, 1824 and died September 2, 1876 and is buried at Gordon Cemetery. Johann Heinrich Birnstiel the son of Karl was born June 27, 1855 and died October 24, 1867, and is buried at Gordon Cemetery. Carl Gebeline (note English spelling of first name) was 65 years of age in the Darke County, Ohio census for 1880. He is listed as a wagon maker. His wife's name is listed as Minnie, aged 40.

The Gift Family

William H. Gift, born in 1839, died in 1913. He was a member of Company E, 87 Ohio Infantry in the Grand Army of the Republic. E. E. Gift, born in 1843, died in 1921. Elmer E. L. son of W. H. & E. died October 17, 1864 - age 11 months, 15 days. All are buried at Gordon Cemetery.

The Gentner Family

Helen [Flory] Rogers married Everett Gentner, born June 10, 1908. He bought the grocery store on Lot 23 and ran it and the post office. For a period of time, Everett's mother, Lew H. "Hattie" Gentner, lived alone in the house beside the store. Everett later sold the store to Carl and Earlene Morris. Everett and Helen had two girls -- Joyce and Phyllis. Joyce Gentner, born March 30, 1948, married Greg Halderman. They have two sons, Brian and Tim. Phyllis, born May 20, 1949, married Russell Skaggs and had a daughter, Sheila. Sheila Skaggs married Robert Lee. Phyllis is divorced.

The Gordon Family

Philip (born July 10, 1788 died September 12, 1857) and Elizabeth [Hayden] Gordon (born November 19, 1782 died August 8, 1863) (both were born in Hunterdon County, New Jersey) built a home just east of the present town of Gordon on the highest elevated section in that area. The purchased the land from Jacob Emmons (see first page 7) for the princely sum of $1,500. Philip Gordon is of Scotch lineage. Henry Gordon (born in 1825 died in 1914), father of Frank S. Gordon (born March 5, 1861) arrived in Miami County Ohio in 1838. He moved from there to Darke County. He was a farmer and married Miss Nancy Owen (born in 1825 died in 1861) who was of Welsh lineage. Nancy's family came from the "rock-ribbed" county of Wales. They settled in Virginia and later members of the family migrated to Knoxville, Tennessee and from there came to Twin Township, Darke County, Ohio. Nancy died in Twin Township in 1862. Henry and Nancy are buried at Gordon Cemetery. A railroad was surveyed and built near the farm. A station house was built there and it was named "Gordon" in appreciation for the many services Philip Gordon provided the railroad. At this time (1849) the railroad was called the "Cincinnati & Miami Rail Road" and is shown on the map of Gordon when it was platted. A church (Baptist shown on a map dated 1857) and cemetery was established on their land. Philip and

Elizabeth are buried at Gordon Cemetery. Frank S. Gordon, son of Henry Gordon, "spent his boyhood days in the town of Gordon where he mastered the rudiments of an English education in the common schools under the direction of Professor J. T. Martz." In September 1884, Henry S. Gordon married Miss Etta McCaughey, daughter of Rev. William McCaughey, a Presbyterian of Darke County. They had two children, Ralph F. Gordon and Virginia E. Gordon. Ralph and Etta were members of St. Paul's Episcopal Church. Mary Gordon, daughter of Philip and Elizabeth Gordon, married John Karr. Their son, Franklin Sylvester Karr was born June 23, 1864. His paternal grandparents, James and Elizabeth Karr, moved from New Jersey, in 1835, and located on a farm in Preble County, where Baltimore (Verona) now stands. Dulcena "Cena" Gordon, a housekeeper, and her widowed mother, Sarah, lived in a two story home on Lot 30 in 1910 and Dulcena was still living there when Helen Flory moved to town in 1920. Dulcena Gordon died and was buried at Ithaca Cemetery on July 27, 1933 at age 79. Her will was signed October 1, 1927 at Greenville and nearly all of the estate goes to cousins and only one Gordon resident, William Rice received $100, was mentioned. Everyone had moved or lived in other communities.

The Grau Family

John A. Grau was a wagon maker living in Gordon with his wife, Rosan and children David, Mary, John, Lewis and Elizabeth when the 1860 census was taken. The Grau Family are buried at Gordon Cemetery. (Some census listed this family as "Graw.")

The Gunder Family

William Gunder laid our or platted the town of Arcanum just before Gordon was platted. William is shown on the 1830 and 1850 census. William died on October 13, 1863 – age 63 years, 6 months and 5 days. Nancy, his wife, died September 20, 1880 when she was 38 years and ten days old. John G. Gunder, son of William and Nancy died October 6,

1850 when 7 years, 10 months and 13 days old. Martin Gunder died April 20, 1865 at age 40 and his wife, Ann E. (1832-1892) are buried at Ithaca Cemetery. Frances C. daughter of Martin and Ann, died June 14, 1865 – age 4 months and 9 days. Harry Gunder and family lived in Gordon in the Edward Ammon store building in the 1930 -1940's time period. Before moving to that location, they lived in the Levi Ammon homestead just south of the Ed Ammon store. It was the finest house in Gordon and sported a turret and still does. Some people said it was a small mansion. Harry Gunder and wife Vergie had four children. Marion, Allen, William "Bill" and Shirley. Marion, Allen and Bill were born in this house and Shirley was born in the Ed Ammon store building. Harry Gunder was a laborer but also went into the chicken hatchery business at the Levi Ammon home with the deluxe turret. They used the barn and some of the Ed Ammon store as a chicken hatchery. The business was named, "Gunder's Hatchery." Vergie Gunder died and was buried at Ithaca Cemetery at age 67 on December 30, 1954. Harry Gunder is buried beside Vergie and next to their son, Allen. The Gunders moved into the Edward Ammon store building and lived there when I knew them. I remember sheets strung on lines separating space into rooms. I remember walls lined with shelving where Ammon's merchandise sat until sold. Marion married Donna Irene Sclaff from Oklahoma. They had two sons. For a time they lived in the old Henry Myers barbershop, but moved back to Oklahoma where they divorced. Marion next married Alice [Cummins] Laxly in 1953 and raised his son Donne. Marion and Alice lived in Arcanum in the general location that his more famous relative, William Gunder, had lived when he platted Arcanum. William "Bill" Gunder married Carolyn Kay Ehlers in 1955. They had one daughter. They presently live in Arcanum, Ohio. Shirley Gunder married Clinton Calvin Stamps in 1957. They had two boys and two girls. Alan, Karmnela, Kevin and Kandis. Shirley lives in Fairborn, Ohio.

The Guy Family

In the 1880 census, Catharine Guy was a widow. She had three sons, Frank, who was a farmer, William and Leo, and one daughter, Cora.

William became a farmer and married Sarah. They had three daughters, Sarah A., 24, Emma 18, and Alice 15. Leo Guy became a barber on Main Street in Gordon and is also listed as having a grocery store on Main Street. Samuel Guy's wife's name was Harriet. They also lived in Gordon. He was a laborer.

The Hall Family

In the 1910 Darke County Ohio Census, Hiram Hall and his wife Elizabeth lived in Gordon. Hiram was a plasterer. Delmer E. Hall lived on Scott Street, on Lot 33, with his wife, Marian in the late 1940s and 1950s. They had two children, Beverly and Roseanna Davy. Delmer had a limp when he walked. Delmer worked for many years as a mechanic at Troutwine Auto Company in Arcanum. I bought my first car from him. It was a 1935 Chevy that had "mechanical" brakes and took forever to get stopped.

The Hanes Family

John Hanes was a farmer and lived on Lot 2 on North Street. John Hanes was the Mayor of Gordon, Ohio in 1936. In later years, John got married. Helen [Flory] Gentner believes John, who was never married, was at least 75 years of age when he got married for the first time. John was happy, at least at first, but began to mumble about marriage. He told Helen Gentner that his new wife, Blanche, thought money grew on trees. John Hanes died and was buried at Ithaca Cemetery on December 18, 1947 at age 86. Mary Eichelbarger, a sister to John, Harley, Roscoe, and Dewey Hanes, all lived at the some place on North Street. Dewey died and was buried at Ithaca Cemetery on age 71 on June 6, 1970. Roscoe died and was buried at Ithaca Cemetery on December 11, 1994 at age 92. The Hanes Woods was part of the 14 acres of ground that went with the Hanes homestead. For many years the "Virginia Reunion" was held there, and many other large reunions were held at this site.

The Hangen Family

The Hangen family lived where Charles "Ezra" and Laura Fourman lived in North Street beside the railroad tracks. The official address is 417 North Street. Don and Naomi Hangen had five children, Karon, Sharon, Denise, Cindy and John. The Hangens left Gordon in August 1977 and moved to Arcanum, Ohio. Don is deceased. Naomi lives in Arcanum. Ohio. Karon married Bob Riesley of Pitsburg in 1988. Karon lives in Pitsburg, Ohio. Sharon [Hangen] Wellbaum has two children, Dawn [Wellbaum] Garlitz and Matthew. The parents are divorced. Sharon lives in Arcanum, Ohio. Denise [Hangen] Swabb married Gary Swabb at the Gordon Methodist Church in July 1972. They have two daughters, Shanda and Aharyn. They live in Arcanum, Ohio. Cindy [Hangen] Reeves had one daughter, Amanda. Cindy lives in Arcanum, Ohio. She is divorced. John Hangen married October 5, 1985 Jolene Rismiller and had three daughters, Jessica, Jayme and Jenna. John lives in Rochester, Wisconsin.

The Hardon Family

Jonathan Hardon died April 13, 1863 at age 60 and is buried at Gordon Cemetery. Jonathan and D. S. Albright had a store and dealt in grain on Lot 27 on Main Street in Gordon.

The Harleman Family

Zebulan Harleman kept a dry goods store and was married to Mary Harleman and they lived on Lot 27 in Gordon and are shown on an 1875 map of town. They had two daughters, Melissa 11, Martha 4 and one son, Charles. Joseph "Joe" Harleman born 1899, died in 1947 and is buried at Ithaca Cemetery, and Freda Louise [Reed] Harleman, born in 1905, died in 1970 had four boys and two girls. The family lived at their home on Lot 5. Bobby was the oldest boy and there was Gale and Byron "Dutch" and Richard "Dick." The two girls were Betty and Janet. Bobby Lowell

Harleman, born March 22, 1926, died July 15, 1985, married September 3, 1950 Alice Mae [Fellers] Harleman, born August 28, 1928, daughter of D. Merlin Fellers. Their children are Deborah Elaine [Harleman] Taylor, born February 25, 1952, married October 20, 1979 to James B. Taylor. Harold Leonard Harleman, born January 27, 1953, married September 8, 1973 Deborah Jo Lephart. Mary Catherine Harleman, born May 7, 1955. David Edward Harleman, born May 26, 1959, married May 3, 1986 Brenda Campbell. And Neal Allen Harleman, born November 16, 1968, married in 1991 Rhonda [Miller] Harleman. Alice lives on Lot 16 and Neal lives on Lot 27. Gale Deo Harleman, born December 19, 1927, died October 16, 1989, married December 24, 1947 Joy Ann Pearson, born November 25, 1929, the daughter of Charles and Eunice Pearson. Their children are Joseph Arthur Harleman, born April 14, 1949, married December 20, 1969, Ellen Robinson. Thomas Lee Harleman, born November 20, 1952 married July 16, 1972, Linda Hines. Scott Lynn Harleman, born January 3, 1955, married January 6, 1974, Brenda Jones. And Janet Eileen [Harleman] Poole, born August 16, 1957, married September 2, 1978, Tommy Poole. Betty Jane [Harleman] Shepard, born December 18, 1929, married July 22, 1950, Roger Allen Shepard, born December 11, 1928, died June 3, 1981, the son of Oscar Ora Shepard and Mildred Ilo [Peden] Shepard. Their children are Rex Allen Shepard, born January 12, 1957. Lisa Lynn [Shepard] Parker, born August 12, 1959, married July 22, 1978 John Randolph Parker. Craig Eric Shepard, born August 6, 1963, married April 18, 1987 Sherry Faye West. And Lori Ann Shepard, born December 3, 1964 lives in the Harleman home on Lot 8 in Gordon, Ohio. Betty lives on State Route 722. Byron Eugene Harleman, born May 17, 1931, married July 22, 1966 Karen Vitatoe. They had Christina Lynette Harleman, born March 9, 1967 married July 18, 1987, Brad Meddock. And Brian Eugene Harleman, born August 8, 1971. Byron remarried Wilma Nadine [Debolt] Harleman and presently lives in Union City, Ohio. Janet Elenora [Harleman] Harshbarger, born March 4, 1933, married March 7, 1953 Donald Wayne Harshbarger, born March 28, 1933. Their children are Robin Lynette [Harshbarger] Anderson, born July 7, 1954, married October 2, 1976 Kenneth Anderson. Dona Key [Harshbarger] Chapman, born August 18, 1955, married May 25, 1975 Timothy Chapman. And Kimbal Alan Harshbarger, born October 15, 1956. Janet lives in Dayton. Richard Dwaine Harleman, born January 14,

1935, died July 30, 1965, married August 18, 1961 Donna Roberts the daughter of Stuart and Ruth Roberts. Their child is Adrienne Lee Harleman, born July 30, 1962. He was a helicopter pilot. Richard is buried at Ithaca Cemetery. Freda Harleman remarried Merlin Fellers. Freda died in 1970.

The Harshbarger Family

Dave and his wife, Sarah [Hemmerich] Harshbarger lived on North Street on Lot 2. They were neighbors to the Ralph and Olive Ary family. David and Sarah Harshbarger lived in Gordon, Ohio in 1920.

The Hart Family

Carolyn Hart, a widow, lived on East Street on Lot 42. I could never find out any more about this lady. She is mentioned in census reports, but that's all. I included her so she would not be forgotten.

The Hartman Family

Amanda Hartman, age 67, lived in Gordon with her son, Samuel, 26, who was a laborer. Her daughter, Laura C., 25, was a tobacco worker.

The Hemmerick Family

Frederick Hemmerick arrived in Gordon in 1849, the same year the town was platted by David Lair. (The name is listed as "Hemrick" in the 1880 Darke County, Ohio Census. He is listed as 45 and his wife, Catherine [note spelling] was 48.) His wife's name was Catharine and she was 68 when the Darke County Census for 1910 was taken, and Fred was 65. Fredrick and Catherine had daughters Sarah E., Mary J., Rebeca

(Rebecca) A., Margaret E., Catie (Katy) A., and Emmie M., and sons, William H., and John S. On the 1920 Darke County Ohio Census, Fred is listed as a foreign national from Germany, and in that year he was living with David and Sarah Harshberger (Harshbarger?).

The Hendrickson Family

Elsie, Gloria and Ray, a student, all live in the sound end of Gordon and are shown on a Gordon Directory for 1910. I was not able to learn any more about this family. I suppose they only lived in the area for a short period of time and moved elsewhere.

The Henninger Family

George M. Henninger, born November 19, 1806 died August 17, 1882 - age 77-8-28 and his wife Mary B. born August 20, 1808 died June 14, 1886 - age 77-9-24. Henninger, George son of H. & R. died November 16, 1856 - age 24-1-7. Frederick son of H. & R. died January 16, 1857 - age 22-1-6. Fridaricker daughter of H. & R. died September 10, 1858 - age 7-5-3. Henninger, Luella daughter of J. & M. died January 22, 1883 - age 11 months 2 days. All are buried at Gordon Cemetery.

The Hipple Family

Henry Hipple was born in 1813 and died in 1894, and his wife, Elizabeth was born in 1825 and died in 1891. They had two children, Mary and John. Henry, Elizabeth and Mary are buried at Gordon Cemetery. John H. Hipple was a newsboy in Gordon. At that time, there were two newspapers delivered each day in town. The Journal came in the morning. Roy Flory (Helen's brother) had one newspaper route and John had the other. Roy helped John deliver his newspapers as John Hipple was blind. Mary Hipple, John's sister, was a housekeeper who lived on East Street with him. Mary had a son, Eddie W. Larmer

The Hofacker Family

Delbert Hofacker, born April 5, 1934 in Preble County, Ohio, and his wife Mary Lou [Hoke] Hofacker, born February 25, 1935, moved to Gordon, Ohio in March 1956, and bought Frank Rhodehamel's garage that had been made over into a home by Joe Hoke. This was located on Lot 7 of the Brown Addition. They lived in this building until Delbert built a more substantial home using cement blocks. When that was completed, the family moved in. They had Brenda Elaine [Hofacker] Little, born March 4, 1963 and David John Hofacker, born December 29, 1966. In August 1968, Delbert and his wife sold this property and moved to a new brick home just at the east edge of Gordon on State Route 722 where they still live. Delbert's parents are Dwight H. Hofacker, born May 2, 1903 and his mother is Sadie I. [Clegg} Hofacker, born November 15, 1907. Delbert's brothers are Stanley M., born 1929, John A., born January 20, 1945 (deceased), Donald Ray, born April 17, 1948, Mildred, born May 3, 1932, Lois, born March 24, 1940, and Doris, born July 15, 1942. Mary Lou's parents are Bernadine N. [Knecht] Hoke and Clarence Hoke, Sr.

The Hoff Family

The Hoff family lived next to the old Methodist Church on east Centre Street (The old church building has been the town hall for as long as I can remember). Susie Miller previously owned the home and prior to that, it was the home of Hol and Ethel O'Dell. Mrs. Hoff later married Dale Lock from Verona and eventually moved there. The youngest girl in the family was Nancy. Nancy [Hoff] Chrisman married John Chrisman, and after twenty years of marriage he died from a heart attack and was buried at Ithaca Cemetery. They had one son. She next married Stanley Hofacker and they live in Greenville. Marie [Hoff] Howard lives in Gettysburg, Ohio. Glenna [Hoff] Creech lives in West Alexandria, Ohio. Ruth [Hoff] Allen lives in Rochester, Minnesota. I used to see Nancy [Hoff} Hofacker at auctions and sales, but have not seen her in recent months.

The Hoffman Family

Otto Hoffman and his wife, Leah, live on East Street with sons John and Harry and daughter Lucille Hoffman (1910 Gordon Directory). I received a letter from Lucille [Hoffman] Weaver in February 1996 when she was then 90 years of age. She drew a map of Gordon as she remembered it and put the names of people she remembered from Gordon. She was in the Bretherns Home in Greenville in 1996. She had at least one daughter, Patricia [Weaver] Sacketl.

The Hoke Family

Joseph "Joe" Hoke and his wife, Laura "Lottie" [Odum] Hoke, the daughter of Robert Odum and Maude [Cassel] Odum lived in Gordon, Ohio on North Street, on Lot 1 from August 4, 1952 until Lottie sold out 43 years later in 1995. Joe was born August 10, 1901 and died June 22, 1988. Joe was the town barber for a number of years and cut hair in a shop on the west side of the house. Lottie was born on January 4, 1921 and presently (1998) lives in West Manchester, Ohio. They have two sons, Joseph "Joe" Hoke Jr., born August 27, 1947 and Floyd Hoke, born April 12, 1957. Joe Hoke Jr., married Gloria [Niswonger] Hoke and had one son, Joseph Eugene Hoke. Joe's current wife is Dana [Musser] Hoke. Floyd Lee Hoke married Tracy [Hobblitt or Hoblit] Hoke and they live in Brookville, but have no children. They bought the house on North Street from George Myers. Joe bought the grocery store on Lot 13 on Main Street that had been in operation since the town was platted from Merle Armitage after her husband, Vern died. He paid $1,700 for the building and lot. At one time, his son, Joe and his wife, Gloria [Niswonger] Hoke, lived in the living quarters attached to the rear of the house. Cleo Hoke and Goldie [Rhoades] Hoke lived on Lot 1 and 2 in Gordon. They moved to Gordon in the summer of 1955. They opened the old Hol O'Dell garage and called it, "Gordon Car Wash." Cleo built a new home on North Street beside Hol O'Dell's garage for his family. They lived in the original O'Dell home on Lot 2 that was a smaller house. When the new house was finished, the family moved in and the small house was sold to Chester "Bud" and Edith Fenton and daughter Marjorie (see Fenton). Cleo and Goldie had several children. Ronald J. Hoke, born January 1, 1941, Lewis F. Hoke, born June 23, 1935, and Betty l [Hoke] Paulus, born June 3, 1939. Ronald or "Ronnie" Hoke worked in the garage in Gordon. The home and station was sold to Tom Knick and his family who are the present owners (see Knick). After Goldie Hoke died, and after his brother, Joe had died, Cleo and Joe's widow, Lottie, got married. The marriage did not last long and the couple were divorced. Ronald J. Hoke, born January 1, 1941, married Barbara J. [Blankenship] Hoke, born April 20, 1945. Barbara's parents are Sarah J. [Clark] Blankenship and Oscar C. Blankenship. Alma [Griffith] Cordell, wife of Perry Cordell, and the sister of Esta (Griffith) Flory, lived in Gordon at the Ezra Fourman home, and in a garage converted into a home by Joe Hoke. It was sold to Delbert Hofacker and from there Alma spent 17 years with Joe and Lottie Hoke, in an apartment in Joe's garage that he made. She moved to Centerville with her son, Carl, after her health began to decline.

The Holt Family

Elizabeth Holt lived in the house on Lot 36 beside the Baptist Church in 1875. Earlier, in 1857, C. W. Holt lived in a home on Lot 49 on East Street.

The Honadle Family

An 1875 Map of Gordon shows Nicholas Honadle as owning the unnumbered lot beside the railroad. It is the largest lot in town bordering the railroad and North Street. His wife, Elizabeth died when she was only 38 years of age. She is buried with Nicholas at the Lutheran Cemetery in Ithaca and died September 2, 1872. Nicholas is also buried at the

Lutheran Cemetery in Ithaca. He was born in 1825 and died in 1914.

The Hosbrook Family

John Hosbrook lived in Gordon, Ohio with his wife, Mary E. They had one daughter, Gertrude E. Hosbrook. She was 17 in the 1910 Darke County Ohio Census. John was an "electric car engineer."

The Howard Family

Milton Howard and his wife, Margaret, lived in Gordon, on West Street (Marilyn Robinson lives there 1998) in a home they built after living on Railroad Street and renting from Abe and Pat Lincoln.

The Howell Family

Furman and Juanita [Fugate] Howell lived in the house I was born in on Railroad Street (Lot #5 Post Addition). They had three children. Connie, Linda and Dorrance "Dorney". Juanita was born January 8, 1923. She lives in West Manchester, Ohio. Furman Howell is buried at New Paris, Spring Lawn Cemetery. Douglas Gayle Howell, born August 20, 1943, is buried at New Paris Cemetery. Dorrance Kaye Howell, born July 24, 1941, is not married. He lives on Miller's Fork Road. Connie Sue [Howell] Hemmerich, born January 31, 1946, is married to Jerry Hemmerich. They had one boy, and one girl. Connie lives in Indiana. Linda Paulette [Howell] Johnson, born February 25, 1950, is married to Bob Johnson. They have three girls. Linda lives in Indiana.

The Idel Family

David Idel was the son of Jacob and Elizabeth Idel. David married the daughter of John and Catherine Karr, Mary Karr. They had two children, daughter Idella and son, Earlen James (1900 Darke County Census). Jacob and Elizabeth Idel had four children: Christena, David, William and Mary (mother of Ralph Burris). Earlen "Earl" or "Jim" Idel and Bertha [Poe] lived on the edge of town on North Street at the corporation limits. Their daughter, Grace [Idel] married Earl Fisher.

The Jones Family

John Sam Jones and his wife, Emma, and their children, Welthy G., Paul S., Edith M., Lucille A., Jeanette J., Margaret and Harry lived in Gordon and appear in the Darke County Ohio Census for 1910. They ran the meat market and restaurant in Gordon. John S. Jones (Emma, and their children, Welthy G., Paul S., Edith M., Lucille A., Jeanette J., Margaret and Harry) owned the "best restaurant in town" and also a meat market on Main and Perry Streets. Sam was a respected citizen and elected to the post of town Trustee on April 5, 1901. W. W. Pierce, Trustee Board President signed the declaration. By the 1920 Census, Emma was a widow still running the restaurant and boarding house.

The Karr Family

John and Mary [Gordon] Karr had one son, Franklin Sylvester Karr. They lived on the homestead just east of Gordon. Franklin was born June 23, 1864 at home. His grandparents, James and Elizabeth Karr, from New Jersey, came to Preble County, Ohio in 1835 and lived on a farm where Baltimore (Verona) now stands. He is buried in Tillman Cemetery, Harrison Township, Preble County, Ohio. Elizabeth Karr was visiting her daughter, some years later, in Michigan and died. She is buried near Niles, Michigan. James Karr was a "valuable guide to newcomers from other states who were looking for suitable sites for their pioneer homes." John Karr, was born in New Jersey, May 25, 1815 and died January 15, 1872. His wife, Mary [Gordon] Karr was born January 25, 1819, and died November 17, 1892. Both are buried at Gordon

Cemetery. John and Mary had six children. All were born in the Karr homestead house. The children were: Elizabeth Ann, married A. A. McElwaine. Elizabeth died February 1, 1875 and is buried beside her parents. Zephaniah Selby, was born September 5, 1844, died May 11, 1872; Rachel Jane, born September 2, 1852, died the same day as her sister, Elizabeth, February 1, 1875; John Iser, born March 31m 1858, died October 22, 1860; Sarah Emma, born March 16, 1860, died April 13, 1878; Franklin Sylvester, the youngest child, born, June 23, 1864. Franklin S. Karr married Miss Sarah E. Nickle, March 25, 1883. She was born in Darke County, Twin Township, on May 16, 1863, daughter of John and Catherine [Dancer] Nickle. John Nickle was born in Wurtemburg, Germany, July 4, 1820. He started for America in May, 1852 aboard a sailing vessel which took months to cross, and landed in New York in August. He lived in Hamilton for a short time and there married Catherine Dancer, also a native of Wurtemburg, born in 1822. John Nickle died June 15, 1899 and his wife, Catherine, died November 6, 1898 and are buried in Twin Township Cemetery. John and Catherine had three children. Amelia, born January 17, 1855, wife of David Sutterbeck of Twin Township (Sluterbeck?); Mary Ann, born August 13, 1859, wife of David Idle, residing near Gordon, and John Henry, born November 1, 1866, who died at age nine years. Franklin S. Karr and Sarah had nine children. Ibbie Jane, born January 29, 1884, married Charles Baker. They have three children: Cora Hazel, Delbert and Orlan Otho. Charles Curtis, born May 29, 1885, married Hazel Corwin, October 9, 1909 and they have two children: Corwin LeRoy and Susie Evelyn. Emma Hazel, born December 18, 1886, married Edward Mattris on January 1, 1912. Cora Ann, born July 21, 1888. Married Harry B. Falknor on October 16, 1912. They had one child: Richard Karr. Ija Gordon, born March 25, 1890. Maude Belle, born June 6, 1892. Married Ralph Aubrey Hart, a teacher of Darke County, on August 9, 1913. Ellie May, born February 27, 1894. John Russell, born September 24, 1898. Graduated from the district school (now torn down) near his home in 1914. John R. Karr was the farmer that I knew when I lived in Gordon, Ohio. I have one good photograph of him with one of his large dogs.

The Kauffman Family

Melinda [Shepard] Kauffman and Tim Kauffman live in Gordon, Ohio. Melinda was born December 4, 1971 at Wayne Hospital in Greenville, daughter of Carol [Shepard] Ritz and Larry Ritz. Tim Kauffman's parents are Patsy [Ware] Kauffman and Ron Kauffman. Melinda and Tim have two sons, Levi born September 15, 1996 and Josef Kauffman born February 7, 1998. Melinda's sisters are Sheryll Ritz, born March 28 and Peggy [Ritz] Dill born March 18.

The Kitt Family

Bryan Kitt was from Ireland. He was 42 when he kept a saloon in Gordon. His wife, Hannah, 35, was also from Ireland. They had one girl living with them whose name was Anna Erwin. She was 12 and from Canada. Bryan Kitt is listed as 53 years of age in the 1880 Darke County census for Twin Township. His wife is now listed as Ann, age 47 (Is this the Anna Erwin above?). They have a daughter, Elizabeth, aged 12. He is out of the saloon business and is listed as a laborer.

The Klink Family

Robert V. Klink married Helen [Woodbury] Klink and had two daughters, Judith and June. Robert was self-employed as a carpenter. Bob and Helen are both deceased.

The Knick Family

Joyce Mills married Tom Knick. They have three children. Steve lives in Xenia, Shannon [Knick] McCullough lives on State Route 722 and Shane Knick lives in Dayton, Ohio.

The Kronenberg Family

Jack Kronenberg and his family lived in Gordon in the last house on the north side of the North Street heading west towards Ithaca. It was the Ella Eller property in 1910. They had two children, Jack and Janet. Janet is deceased but Jack is living in California. Jack's father ran a tiny gas station there (there was one hand gasoline pump) and he did some auto repairs in the garage behind the station. They sold soft drinks, candy bars and chances on punch-out tickets. He was also an inventor and one of the inventions I remember was a key-like device that slipped on the end of a tube of toothpaste and when turned would squeeze out the last bit of toothpaste from the tube. Jack's mother left her husband and married the farmer who lived in the Philip and Elizabeth Gordon house, John Stump. Shortly after this, the Kronenberg family moved from town. Jack Kronenberg was older than me. After he moved and grew up, he married Thelma Bright who was from Pitsburg, Ohio. They are both alive and live in California.

The Lafferty Family

Hugh. H. Lafferty (Lefferty possible spelling in 1910 Census) was the Methodist Church minister from 1908 until replaced in 1910 by J. F. Probst. His family lived on East Street -- Mary, his sister, and Juliette aged 77 (widowed) lived with him.

The Lage Family

William "Bill" Lage (pronounced "log - ee") married Ruth Rice in 1916. Bill was born in Germany in 1891 (see footnote) and Ruth was born in 1896. She died in 1984 and Bill died after Ruth. They never had any children. After they were married, they moved in with Ruth's parents, Tommy and Sarah "Ella" Rice, on Main Street. Bill was born in Germany. Bill was an excellent mechanic on cars and trucks. He owned and operated a garage and sold new Reo automobiles from his shop on

Main Street on Lot 14 (the building is still there and owned by Jack Foland). They also sold gasoline from hand pumps. After he stopped selling Reos, Bill always bought new Chevrolets from Troutwine's in Arcanum. During the Second World War, Bill and Ruth bought "Victory Garden" seeds from me each year that I sold them. Tommy Rice, Ruth's father, bought "Cloverine" salve from me when I sold that from door to door. They were my best customers in town. Most people saved garden seed from year to year, but Lage's always bought fresh seed from me. Bill also owned the bulk gasoline business and a driver delivered gasoline to service stations in the area during the 1930s, 40s and 50s. It became a Pure Oil Distribution Company in later years. The truck also delivered fuel oil to farmers and independent stations. Bill owned the Ezra Post Farm at the west edge of town and a farm north of West Sonora. He might have owned other farms in the area. Mr. and Mrs. William Lage, of Gordon, left their entire estate to the Wayne Hospital in Greenville, Ohio. A memorial plaque is installed in the hospital. The bequest was the largest the hospital ever received according to published reports.

The Lair Family

On the 20th day of May 1839, Philip Gordon left his ancestral home in New Jersey to become a pioneer settler in what was then known as "the far west" State of Ohio. With him came Elizabeth [Harden] Gordon, his wife, his sons, Andrew and Henry and David and Sarah [Gordon] Lair. Sarah was born November 19, 1813. Sarah and David had Henry Lair, a veteran of the War of 1861. He lived in West Milton, Ohio. Joseph Lair, a veteran of the Civil War and married but had no children. David Lair was a harness maker. He was responsible for platting Gordon, Ohio and did it in 1849 (I have a copy of the plat map and surveyor's statement). It reads as follows: "The Town of Gordon is laid out in the North part of the East half of the North East quarter of Section 35 in Township Eight of Range 3 East. The Streets of said Town run North & South and East and West crossing at right angles, the lots are numbered consecutively from 1 to 27 and are 1 chain and 25 links in front and 2 chains deep except fractional Lot 27 the length of the boundaries of which are designated on the plat the width of the several streets is shown on that, a stone is set at the N. W. corner of Lot 21 which bears from the N. W. corner of said half quarter of 26 35' & 56 links October 17th., 1849. John Wharry, Sur. Darke County Ohio. "To all to whom these presents shall come — Know ye that I David Lair have laid and established the Town of Gordon in the County of Darke and State of Ohio, conformally to the within plat and notes thereof, signed by the surveyor of said County. "In witness I have hereto set my hand and seal the 17th of October A. D. 1849. signed David Lair. Executed in the presence of, signed John G. Hutten, signed John Wharry." David Lair was a harness maker and lived on Main Street and Perry. His widow, Sarah [Gordon] Lair was still living in the home in 1910, listed as a widow. In a 1911 newspaper clipping, it reported that she died after a fall at her house. The newspaper said she was "about 87 years of age," but if she was born in 1813, she would have been 98 in 1911 when she died. John Mathias Lair, was listed, with David Lair, on the 1850 census of Twin Township, Darke County, Ohio. Samuel Lair and his wife, Ann, lived in Gordon. They had two children, Laura and Katy. Samuel was a day laborer.

The Lambert Family

Jacob A. Lambert and his wife, Lizzie, (Elizabeth?) lived in Gordon with their son, Walter J. and daughters, Sada E., and Mabel Lambert. Jacob was a butcher. Peter Shilling, a butcher, lived with the family.

The Lauver Family

John and Dorothy, lived along the railroad tracks south of town -- at the corporation limits. They had a small farm. They had one daughter, Phyllis. John Lauver was born December 25, 1894 and passed away on October 19, 1959 and is buried at Ithaca. He was born in Preble County and was 64. Dorothy [Warts] Lauver was born October 23, 1913 and died January 10, 1996. She was born in Darke County and was 82. She was buried at Ithaca Cemetery on January 13, 1996. Phyllis [Lauver] Michael married Gerald R. Michael from Middletown, Ohio. He was born in September 8, 1943. They got married in Ithaca, Ohio on May 11, 1968. They have three children. Steven A. Michael was born at Middletown, Ohio on December 4, 1969. Brenda A. [Michael] Hickman was born October 17, 1971. She married Paul Hickman and they are living in Middletown, Ohio. Deborah S. Michael was born on May 21, 1977. The family lives in Lebanon, Ohio.

The Lawson Family

William "Bill" Lawson and his wife, Barbara lived in Gordon and had three sons, Jeff, Mark and Eddie Lawson.

The Layton Family

John Layton was a dealer in general merchandise, and boots and shoes, on Main Street, Lot 13, in 1857.

The Leisure Family

Oscar E. Leisure and his wife, Eva Jean lived on East Street on Lot 39. They had two children, Delores and Guy. Oscar was a Track man for the railroad. Jeanette Barge lived with them and went to school at Gordon.

The Lincoln Family

While working in Dayton as a housekeeper for a family, Vivia Elizabeth May Ballengee, born in 1909, read an advertisement in the newspaper about a man, in Clayton, Ohio, who wanted to hire a housekeeper. She went to work for Lurton Clarence Lincoln, born December 24, 1877. He was employed by Dayton Power and Light Company and recently divorced from his first wife, Myrtle [Straw] Lincoln (originally from

Eaton, Ohio). He was living in Clayton, Ohio at the time (early 1930s). Lurton Clarence Lincoln and Vivia E. Ballengee got married and had one son, Abraham. Abraham was born in Gordon, Ohio on October 25, 1934 when the clock was striking twelve noon. I was delivered with the assistance of a midwife, Emma Shoenfelt. Emma also suggested my parents name me, "Abraham" since I am President Lincoln's third cousin, three times removed. The marriage did not last long and Vivia and Lurton "Lurt" divorced. For the rest of his life, Lurton worked as a Packer for Simonds Worden and White Company, in Dayton. The company made grinding wheels and knives. Dad's last wife was named Marie. She moved to Bradford after my father died. Lurton Clarence Lincoln died on June 25, 1955 and is buried in the old cemetery in Eaton (Union). Vivia died January 4, 1998 and is buried in El Campo, Texas. Abraham Lincoln lived on Railroad Street from 1934 until the family moved to Greenville. He returned when he was 16 to live with his father on Main Street next to the Gentner Grocery Store and Post Office. After a three year tour of duty in the U. S. Army in Japan, Abraham returned to Ohio and married Patricia Ann [Custer] Lincoln, born October 26, 1936 at Lewisburg, Ohio, Preble County, and they lived on Railroad Street in Tommy Rice's blacksmith shop that had been converted into a small home. Pat and Abe were married in Richmond, Indiana on July 12, 1955 by a Justice of the Peace. They borrowed Dwight Ressler's car to make the trip to Richmond, Indiana. After the marriage, Abraham returned to Japan to complete his tour of duty there. He returned to Ohio briefly and with his wife and new baby, Angela, moved to Baltimore, Maryland where they lived in Dundalk, Maryland close to Fort Holabird where he was stationed. Pregnant with Christopher Patrick, Patricia moved back to Arcanum to stay with her family while Abe finished his tour of Army service at Fort Holabird. When he was discharged, the couple moved into the little house on Railroad Street. At the time, Abe worked at National Cash Register Company in Dayton. They had four children while living there. The last child was born while they lived in Brookville, Ohio. Their children are: Angela Beth [Lincoln] Dasner, born June 1, 1956, (married Gary Dasner and had son Alex); Christopher Patrick Lincoln, born May 10, 1957 (married Laurie Patera and had two children, Brittney and Justin Lincoln); Melinda Annette [Lincoln] Napoletano, born July 5, 1958, 1957 (married Keith Napoletano and had son Noah);

Rebecca Sue Lincoln, born March 7, 1962, and Melissa May [Lincoln] Gilliland, born June 27, 1973 (married David Gilliland and had daughter Audrey). Abraham Lincoln would later teach school in Greene County and in Montgomery County at the Joint Vocational School now called Miami Valley Career Technology Center. He also founded Calligrafree and conducted a worldwide business from his home in Brookville, Ohio. He authored over two dozen books on handwriting and calligraphy, was a popular artist and painter, and active in environmental issues. In the 1990s he founded Whiz Bang Graphics and that company has been very active in creating World Wide Web pages for businesses on the Internet. He remains active in Rotary and does a Lot of research work and genealogy from his home office in Brookville, Ohio. Patricia Ann [Custer] Lincoln has gone on to work for Miami Valley Career Technology Center in Adult Education. If you have signed up for an adult class she has probably registered you.

The Little Family

John Little, a farmer, and his wife, Martha, lived in Gordon in 1900 with their daughters, Pearl and Elsa.

The Locke Family

Dale Locke and his wife, Goldie, lived on Main Street. They lived in the home that Cena Gordon had owned and the house the Mowry family would live in. They had two children, Clinton Locke and Lilly Locke. When Goldie died, Dale married Mrs. Hoff, Nancy's mother, who lived on Centre Street on Lot 4 where the first parsonage was located (presently beside the Town Hall).

The Long Family

John Charles Long and his wife Ethel [Augustine] (Ethel's maiden name is shown spelled as above and also 'Augusti.' per her son, Richard C. Long) Long lived on Lot 12 in Gordon in the house David and Sarah Lair once owned. John drove a "huckster" truck for Boyer's Grocery, selling groceries and other merchandise to local farmers. John was born January 7, 1907 and died July 14, 1963. Ethel Long was born December 3, 1910 and died November 13, 1989. Both are buried at a cemetery in Covington, Ohio. When Boyer's store stopped the rural route sales and the huckster truck was sold, John began hauling grain for Frank Rhodehamel. He hauled grain to the John Smith grain elevator in Arcanum, Ohio. They had two children. Richard C. "Dick" and Janet "Jenny" Long. Richard married Lucille M. [Skiver] Long born January 4, 1928, and they had two children. Jon Richard Long born January 22, 1956 (Retired U.S. Army) is single and lives with his parents, and Angela Kay Long born May 7, 1962. Angela Kay [Long] Welch had one son, Dylan Tyler Welch born January 29, 1989. Dick and his wife live in Union City, Ohio. Jenny married a man whose name is Glick. They had 6 children and their names are Sue, Judy, Terry, Pat, Brenda and Timmy. All are married. Jenny's husband deserted them, Jenny wrote to me. There are a total of 32 in Jenny's family. She lives in Dixon, Missouri. My mother would baby-sit Dick and Jenny Long on Saturday nights when their folks, John and Ethel went away to dance. John played in a band for round and square dancers. Mother would make chili so everyone would have plenty to eat when they came home. Dick and Jenny would go along with their folks to these dances in the summer but stayed at home in the winter. Dick remembers that his dad and mom had people over to round and square dance at their house in Gordon and they were all having a good time. He said a lot of people "hollered about it and said we couldn't do it anymore." The family left Gordon and moved to Littles Road near Arcanum. John got a better job at the John Smith grain elevator. Ethel kept their house on Littles Road. John and Ethel are both deceased.

The Longenecker Family

James and his wife, Maude are listed as residents of Gordon, Ohio in the 1936 Directory of Darke County, Ohio, Directory of Gordon.

The Lynch Family

John Lynch and his wife, Ida, had one daughter, Hettie. The Lynch family lived in a nice home on Lot 27. Ida died and was buried at Ithaca Cemetery in 1938 at 74. John W. Lynch died and was buried at Ithaca Cemetery on June 7, 1939 at age 69. This is the present home of Helen [Flory] Gentner. Helen bought the house from the daughter, Hettie Lynch. Hettie died and was buried at Ithaca Cemetery at age 82 on April 27, 1971.

The Marcum Family

Nelson and Catherine [Miller] Marcum had a son, Charles "Sandy" Marcum, on January 17, 1874. He was born at home just east of Gordon. Charles had three sisters and a brother who were also born on the farm. They were Ella, Minnie and Anna, and brother, George. Catherine was listed as a widow in the 1920 Darke County, Ohio Census - she was then 75 years of age. Charles Marcum married Martha [Pace] Marcum and they never had any children. Charles spent his early years in farm work but later "clerked" for Levi Ammon and Sons for 17 years. He built a new store, in 1918, on Main Street and ran that until his death on October 2, 1936 at the age of 62. He passed away at home, on a Friday, following an extended illness (People who knew him have said that he had heart problems). Sandy was buried in Memorial park cemetery in Dayton in 1936. Catherine, Sandy's mother, died and was buried at Ithaca Cemetery at age 82 on April 25, 1927.

The McElwaine Family

Alpheus McElwaine, born June 16, 1835 died September 3, 1911 and his wife Elizabeth A., died February 1, 1875, lived in Gordon, Ohio as late as

1917. Their sons Edward died at the age of 21 years on October 1, 1886 and John died on August 25, 1873. The family are buried at Gordon Cemetery.

The McGraw Family

J. W. S. McGraw lived in a home on Lot 9 in Gordon and is shown on an 1857 map. His occupation was that of a wagon maker. He also owned a blacksmith shop across the street on Lot 8.

The McGriff Family

The McGriff family owned the Sluterbeck home for many years. Clyde McGriff owned the farm. He and his wife, Orpha, had lived on West Street before buying the farm and moving south of town. They had one daughter, Glenna, and one son, Layland. Layland was born on March 18, 1923 and died on January 8, 1996. He is buried at Memorial Oaks Cemetery. Orpha died and was buried at Ithaca Cemetery at age 74 on December 17, 1959. Glenna McGriff married Chester Hutton and later moved to Madrid Avenue in Brookville, Ohio where I met her again. I had known her when she lived on the Sluterbeck farm but she was older than I was and we had no common interests. Clyde and Orpha's son, Layland McGriff had two children, Larry and Carolyn. Larry McGriff lives on Madrid Avenue in Brookville, just around the corner from our house. Carolyn McGriff married Gerald Tebics, and they live on the same street as Larry and his family but going in the opposite direction. They have two children, Chris and Jody. Jody [Tebics] Dickens married Christopher Dickens and they have two sons, Jayme and Joseph Dickens. Clyde's brother was called "Gus" and he lived on Gordon-Landis Road, just northwest of Gordon about a half mile. His farm adjoined the town on the west side. In later years, the Synder family lived there. Gus McGriff and Clyde McGriff are first cousins to Helen [Flory] Gentner who still lives in Gordon, Ohio.

The McKinley Family

George N. McKinley, born in 1877, lived in Gordon, Ohio with his wife, Bertha D., born in 1877. They had one daughter, Mary E. McKinley and four sons, William K., Clarence H., Frederick A. and Loren E. McKinley (1910 Census).

The Michael Family

William D. Michael died October 1855. He was 100 years 4 months and fought in the Revolutionary War. His wife, Margaret Michael died in March in 1855 at 74. Both are buried at Gordon Cemetery.

The Mikesell Family

Howard L. Mikesell and his wife, Mardell and daughter, Linda Lou live on Lot 3 Brown's Addition. Howard was a Millwright at Frigidaire in Dayton, Ohio. I was not able to get more information on this family although I tried on several different occasions.

The Miller Family

David Miller was born February 27, 1858 and died on March 3, 1943. His wife was Ella Mae [Brown] Miller who was born on February 23, 1872 and she died on April 10, 1916. Their children were William J. Miller, born October 15, 1899 and died May 30, 1962 was their son. His wife's name was Myrtle Mae. Susie Miller was born on September 11, 1901 and died on April 11, 1990. She never had any children, but her brother, Marvin, said she took care of him like his mother. Treva Irene [Berke] Miller was born June 25, 1905 and died on June 14, 1992. She married Elmer Berke. Denver Miller was born November 23, 1907 and died December 24, 1976. Cleo LeRoy was born July 5, 1910 and died on March 5, 1978. Viola Jeanette Miller was born on March 26, 1913 and died on March 5, 1995. Marvin Monroe Miller was born on March 22, 1916 and was at my office today, May 4, 1998. David Miller's brother was Charles "Charlie" Miller. He and his wife, Carrie "Clara" lived on Lot 17 on Main Street. George Scheiding lived with them and a lady who was nearly blind, Margaret Henninger. (1940s). Cleo Miller and his wife, Vivian, lived along the railroad tracks in a small house on Lot 28. They had two boys. Larry and Roney Dean. Cleo was an engraver at NCR in Dayton. Larry married Mary I. Bazemore and have two daughters, Alice and Elizabeth "Liz." They live in Columbus, Georgia. Roney Dean Miller, born September 1939, married Marilyn [Wickline] Miller. They have two children, Mark and Becky. They lived in what once was the Charles "Buck" Eichelbarger's home in the south end. Roney is a Nazarene pastor. Roney is presently living with Marilyn in Beavercreek, Ohio. His home in Gordon is presently for sale. (1998). Susie Miller lived in a house on Centre Street next to the town hall - a parsonage when first built. Simon Miller and his wife, Lyda lived in town. He was a "horse seller." They had two sons, Charley D. and Elven G., and two daughters, Grace S. and Ruth Miller (1900 Darke County, Ohio Census.)

The George Mills Family

George "Joe" Mills and his wife, Arline, had five children. They lived in town on Lot 14 across from the store and post office on Main Street. Joe is deceased but Arline still lives there. Joe was a Foreman at Simonds Worden and White Company, in Dayton. The company made grinding wheels and knives. George's parents were Arthur Hurbel Mills, born June 24, 1882, died February 4, 1962, at home of George and Arline Mills -- buried in Pyrmont Cemetery. He married Clara May [Riley] Mills. She was born in November 23, 1892 and died on May 30, 1942. She is buried in Pyrmont Cemetery. Arthur Mills was a storekeeper and a farmer. They had eight children. Edna [Mills] Metzger, Harry, Robert, Harley, Walter, George, Charles William, Raymond, born August 8, 1919, died September 16, 1920. Eugene was stillborn April 26, 1924. George and Arline's children are Donna Mills who married Jerry Shepard and moved to Greenville, Ohio. They adopted one boy, Matthew Arthur. Anita Mills married Don Schneider from Louisville, Kentucky. They have two girls, Kate and Karla. Joyce Mills married Tom Knick. They have three children. Steve lives in Xenia, Shannon [Knick] McCullough live on State Route 722 and Shane Knick lives in Dayton, Ohio. Mark W. Mills married Sandra Sue Myers, a high school sweetheart. They have three children -- Julie, Jeff and Joseph. Linda Mills married Dan Holt and they have two daughters, Leah and Lauren, and they live in Tipp City, Ohio.

The William Mills Family

William Eugene Mills, born January 17, 1937 at Trotwood, Ohio, the son of Dorothy Jean [Puterbaugh] Mills, born in Montgomery County, Ohio and Omer Sylvester Mills born in Perry Township, Ohio married Dolores Jean [Heeter] Mills, born July 21, 1937, the daughter of Margaret Lucretia [Gephart] Heeter and Jesse Millard Heeter. William has one sister, Pauline A. [Mills] Rehmert who was born January 30, 1935. The William Mills family lives on the corner of Main and North Street in Gordon, Ohio. This home was, at one time, the home of Esta and Ira Flory who came to town in 1920. Flory ran a restaurant from their home at this home until they moved to Railroad Street. The shop or building next to the alley was the cabinet shop of William Rhodehamel who lived at this address in the late 1930s and through the middle 1940s. Sarah, Bill Rhodehamel's wife, chewed tobacco and smoked Kool Cigarettes. She died there and was buried in Tennessee. Bill worked at the Verona Lumber Company and cut off one finger while using a table.

The Morris Family

Carl and Earlene were farmers for 16 years on the Henry Myers farm east of Gordon. Carl Morris bought the grocery store that Sandy Marcum built from Everett and Helen [Flory] Gentner on Labor Day in1956. At one time or another all of the Morris children worked in the store. Helen continued to work in the store as did Delores [Flory] Bruner. The store was robbed twice. Carl Madison Morris and Ruby Earlene [Netzley]

Morris still live in Gordon beside the grocery store and post office they owned for many years. They had three children. Carl's parents were David L. Morris and Edna [Kindell] Morris. They are both buried at Covington, Ohio. Earlene's parents were Glen Netzley, born August 4, 1897, died November 10, 1948, buried at Greenville Cemetery. Glen's parents were Ira and Forest [Besecker] Netzley. They are both buried at Abbottsville Cemetery. Earlene's mother was Elizabeth Thompson, born November 4, 1893, died March 13, 1986, buried at Greenville Cemetery. Sarah's parents were Urias and Mary [Myers] Thompson, buried at Ithaca Cemetery. Judy Morris married Robert Hocker and they had two children, Roberta and Richard Hocker. (They are now divorced). Roberts parents are Harold and Margaret [Williamson] Hocker. Roberta [Hocker] Bevins married Mike Bevins and they had two children (They are now divorced), Ryan Michael Bevins and Erin Michelle Bevins. Richard Hocker married Letitia [Lambert] Hocker and they had two children. Kylee Ann Hocker and Lakin Nicole Hocker. Her parents are Doug and Barbara [Warner] Lambert. Jane [Morris] Brown married Gary Brown and they had two children, Rhonda Jane and Gary Randall Brown. Gary's parents are Paul and Margaret [Maddock] Brown. Rhonda [Brown] Kress married Joel Kress and they had two children, Tristan Joel (TJ) and Megan Rae. Joel's parents are Eldon and LaRue [McGillvary] Kress. Gary Randall Brown married Rhonda [Smith] Brown and they had two children, Grant Randall and Austin John Brown. Her parents are John D. and Gale [Towsend] Smith. Gene Morris married Nelda [Whiting] Morris and they had three children, Scott A. Morris, Douglas C. Morris and Michael Gene Morris. Scott married Anessa [Sharp] Morris. Her mother is Kay Sharp. They had two children, Ashley Christine (Her mother is Kim [Loxley] Morris) and Mikaela Sharp. Scott recently bought the old John Hanes house in Gordon and with his father's help, is fixing it. Douglas C. Morris married Deanna [Peden] Morris whose parents are Richard and Carol C. Peden. They had three children, Jared Daniel, Kayla Anne and Hallie Ruby. Michael Gene Morris lives in Arcanum, Ohio in a house that he is buying. Michael is 19. Gene Morris and family lives in the home that once belonged to George and Grace Mundhenk, and later to Bob and Helen Klink (Lyman and Mabel Woodbury's daughter).

The Mowry Family

Rodney Anson Mowry born March 21, 1893 died February 10, 1976, and Lillian [Woodall] Mowry born March 2, 1898 died May 22, 1991, moved from Dayton, Ohio to Gordon, in 1936. They bought "Cena" Gordon's old house where the road bends at the south end of Gordon. The Mowrys are buried at Polk Grove Cemetery (West of Vandalia), Butler Township, Montgomery County, Ohio. The Mowry kids called their dad, "Pappy." Rodney worked as a grinder at Acme Pattern Tool Company. The Mowry's had five children. Virginia, Caroline, Roberta, William, and George. Virginia Ruth Mowry born February 24, 1921, in Dayton, Ohio, married Ralph Wogoman, December 21, 1940. Ralph was born September 28, 1919 died December 8, 1997. Ralph's parents were Manuel Wogomon (b. 8/20/1894 d. 8/26/1968) and Clara Elizabeth Baker (b. 8/2/1893 d. 1/24/1973) who are buried at Abbottsville Cemetery. They had two children, Chloe Ann and Doug. Virginia lives near Union City, Indiana. Ralph is deceased. Caroline married and had six children, but was divorced in 1973. She remarried a retired sailor whose name was Ridgeway. They had thirteen years together before he passed away. She lives in California. Caroline drove with her daughter and son-in-law-to-be, all the way from California to be at the Kids from Gordon School Reunion, held in June 1995. Roberta Mae [Mowry] married Elmer Rhodehamel from Gordon in April 1949. They had two children, James Allen Rhodehamel and Mary Ann Rhodehamel. Roberta passed away in August 1972, Elmer passed away in June 13, 1974 and James Allen passed away on August 20, 1974. Mary Ann is the only surviving member of this family and lives in Union City, Indiana. William "Bill" Mowry served in the U.S. Navy and later died and was buried in California. George married Roberta Shell from Lewisburg. They have two children, Rebecca Ann and Scott. George lives with Roberta in Lewisburg, Ohio. Both are retired.

The Moyer Family

Martin and Ida Moyer had two sons, Roy and Harry Moyer. There were two daughters, Edna and Hazel - both were deaf mutes. Edna married a Klepinger. Hazel also married. Roy Moyer was married to Mamie [Bechtol] and had a son, Donovan. Roy died and was buried at Ithaca Cemetery at age 60 in 1952. Mamie O. Moyer died at age 62 and on March 6, 1955 and is buried at Ithaca Cemetery. Donovan's wife's name is Olive. They had several children. Donovan died and was buried at Ithaca Cemetery at age 63 on February 12, 1976. Richard married Linda Ann Riesley from Pitsburg in 1961. Richard works for the Centers for Disease Control and has traveled all over the world. They have two sons, Brad, who is married, and Jeff who was single at age 25. Karen Sue Moyer married Steve Reser in 1982 and has stepchildren, and a son, Brian Moyer, now 33 years old. Cheryl [Moyer] Gray lived in Arcanum. Jane [Moyer] Urlage also lives near Arcanum. Harry Moyer was married and had a son, Paul Moyer. Paul's wife's name was Katherine (or Kathryn). They had a son, Eugene "Gene" Moyer. Gene has been the president of the Lewisburg Board of Education.

The Mundhenk Family

Charles F. "Mont" Mundhenk and wife, Katie, owned the general store in Gordon. He is listed in the 1900 - 1920 Census as a merchant. They had one son, Lawrence. Katie was the postmaster in Gordon for a number of years since the post office was located in the back of his store. The store is on Lot 13. George and Grace (Grace was George's second wife. He was originally married to a lady whose first name was Mollie) lived in Gordon. I have a nice photo of George and Grace when they were older and sitting on the steps of their house. They lived in a home on Lot 6 in Brown's Addition when I knew them in the early 1940s. Grace died and was buried at Ithaca Cemetery at age 67 on October 22, 1947. George died and was buried at Ithaca Cemetery at age 83 on March 2, 1949. Francis M. Mundhenk's wife was named Bertha. They had one son, Marion.

The Myers Family

George and Ida Mae Myers lived on Lot number 1 of the Post Addition along North Street and Railroad Street. They had a large family. George and his wife, Ida May, had Christy Myers, who married Ruth Eubank. Charles married Esther Trump, and Paul married Treva Longenecker. Cecil married Leona Hunt and Luther, married Irene. Harold, married Velma and Merle married Theo Heckman. Claude married Treva Carmony and Willard married Mary Heckathorn. Bessie married Otwin Fourman. George and Ida sat on their small porch on the east side of their home when the weather was nice. I lived south of them on Railroad Street (Lot 5) and when I was small, mother would let me walk to their house to "visit." George liked to eat a handful of freshly ground raw hamburger meat which I thought was really strange. Ida May used to bake sugar cookies and would bring out several for us to eat. I enjoyed eating those cookies and have never tasted another like them. George ran a coal office in town for many years. He also had a coal yard along the east side of the railroad tracks directly across from Lots 3, 4, and 5 on Railroad Street. The cement coal bins were still there when I was a child and lived on Railroad Street. George was portly, gentle, had a pock mocked big nose and rosy red cheeks. He smoked Prince Albert pipe tobacco in the red can. He also drank a lot and was often drunk at home and was abusive to his wife. He died and was buried at Ithaca Cemetery on June 5, 1953. He was 83 years of age. Ida May Myers died and was buried at Ithaca Cemetery on September 6, 1951 at age 78. Henry Myers was married and had a family. He was the barber in Gordon for many years and his shop was located on the corner of Lot 16 where the Weston Warwick hotel had been located. A Town Pump and Water Trough was located there. This was also the lot where the Tommy Rice Blacksmith Shop had been located for a period of time in the 1920s. Henry and Mrs. Myers lived in a house on Lot 15. Sarah Myers is listed as a widow of 73 years of age in a census report on Gordon, Ohio. Paul Myers and his wife, Treva lived next to the railroad tracks on North Street. They had two children, Twila and Lucretia. Paul was a punch press operator at Leland Electric Company. Charles Myers married Esther [Trump] Myers. Their daughter, F. Arline, married George "Joe" Mills.

The Nealeigh Family

John and Elizabeth Nealeigh are listed in the 1860 census for Darke County, Ohio. Henry and his wife Rebecca are listed in the same census. Daniel Nealeigh and wife Mary A. had one child, Francis. 1860 Census for Darke County. William and his wife Rachel had children, Jacob, Mandy, Nackey, Hetty and Julia A. Nealeigh. 1860 Census for Darke County. He was a minister but not at the Methodist Church in Gordon. He was probably a Baptist Minister in Gordon.

The Neff Family

Ivan Neff and his wife, Barbara, live on Lot 33 on Main and Scott Streets in Gordon, Ohio. (1998).

The Norvell Family

Ronald and Sue Norvell have lived in Gordon for a number of years. They live in the home on Lot 15, on Main Street, where Henry Myers, the barber and his wife had lived.

The O'Dell Family

Noah (a veterinary) and Hannah kept a livery stable and sold grain on North Street. They lived in their home on Lot 2 on East Street. Their children, Marion M, son, Amanda C. daughter, Ida, daughter, William H. son, Charles J, son and Carla E. son (1880 Darke County Census and 1900 Census). William H. O'Dell's wife's name was Margaret. No children were listed in the 1880 Darke County Census (1880 Darke County Census). Marvin O'Dell was a veterinary physician (1900 Darke County Census), whose wife was named Anna. They had two children:

Vergie (married Harry Gunder) and Hollie. Anna O'Dell died and was buried at Ithaca Cemetery at age 71 in 1937. Noah and Hannah's son, Marion M. O'Dell was Holly G., or as we called him, "Hol," O'Dell. Hol lived with his wife, Ethel, in the home on Lot 4 on Centre Street. (Marion M. O'Dell became a veterinary like his father and operated in the same livery in Gordon). Hol was a garage mechanic, welder and sold Mobil gasoline from his small station on the corner of North and East Streets. The name of his garage was, "Square Deal Garage." Hol died and was buried at Ithaca Cemetery on December 16, 1949 at age 57. Ethel died and was buried at Ithaca Cemetery at the age of 59 on March 15, 1953. Ethel had the ability to cure people who had been burned by fire by speaking words over them. I saw this happen, when Hol accidentally burned Bud Flory with a welding torch. Ethel and Bud went out of the garage and when he came back the burn was gone. Hol told me that Ethel learned how to do this from her mother. That it was a gift that was only passed down from mother to daughter and that no man was allowed to see it done unless the man was being cured. He had to swear that he would never reveal how it was done or the burn would return and the woman would lose her healing powers. Haner O'Dell was a widow and lived on Perry Street. Henry O'Dell was a farmer whose wife was Elizabeth. They had two children, Sylvanus and Molly (1880 Darke County Census). Sylvanus O'Dell got married. His wife's name was Sarah. They had three daughters: Minnie, Armina, and Eva O'Dell (1880 Darke County Census). Martin S. O'Dell was a laborer whose wife's name was Isidore. They had one son, Orvil (1880 Darke County Census). John O'Dell's wife's name was Sarah. They had four sons, Eli, Emsley, Ira and John, and two daughters, Dela and Sallie O'Dell (1880 Darke County Census).

The Otto Family

Gottleib Otto and his wife, Suffie, lived in Gordon in 1880. He was a shoemaker.

The Overholser Family

Charles Overholser was a physician who lived with his wife and children in a fine home on Lot 21. His wife was Nora. Their children were sons named Sanford and Jerold, and daughter Elizabeth.

The Patterson Family

Willis B. Patterson was the Methodist Church minister at the Methodist Church in 1916. His wife's name was Edna. They had two daughters, Mary and Elizabeth.

The Phillips Family

The 1857 map of Gordon, Ohio shows Mrs. Phillips living on Lot 10 on East Street. Richard Phillips, 41, was a farmer who lived with his wife, Elizabeth H., 37, and daughters, Mary C., 18, Harriet, 16, John M. 15, Rebecca 12, Elizabeth 9 and William 8 months (1860 Darke County, Ohio Census).

The Pierce Family

William W. Pierce, and his wife, Jennie, lived in Gordon, Ohio in 1900. William Pierce, a son of William and Jennie, and two daughters, Susan and Martha. He was a teacher.

The Pinkerton Family

Frank Pinkerton and his wife, Opal [Cashnier], had four children. Frank Jr., Lorean "Peggy," Vivian and David Pinkerton. They owned the grocery store on Main Street that Sandy Marcum had. Frank and Opal are deceased. Lorean Pinkerton married Robert Clark from Arcanum. They had one son, Dennis called "Denny." I went to "Bob and Peg's Belling" after their marriage in Gordon. It was a loud affair — bells ringing, beating on wash tubs and dragging cans behind cars. Lorean's second husband (following a divorce) was to Lloyd Hall. They had one child, Larry. Larry is married and lives in Dayton. Vivian Pinkerton moved to California and married Warren Ball. They have three children, Jon, Janine and Penny. Penny and Jon both live in Texas and Janine lives in California. Frank Jr. got married after a hitch in the Army during the Second World War. He married Charlene. They had five children and one girl. Frank, Gerry, Sam and Bruce all live in Hillsboro. Cherylann "Sherry," the only daughter died May 28, 1978. Frank owned his own business called "Intermatic, Inc." and his brother, David, often worked for him when the business (repairing mechanical timers) was located in Dayton. Junior's wife, Charlene, died September 24, 1995, after coming with Frank to the Kids from Gordon reunion in June 1995. David married Florence and had one son, David, Jr. Florence had one daughter, Marsha. David owned and operated International Service Center on Xenia Avenue in Dayton. The company also repaired timers. David is deceased.

The Plotts Family

Reverend Marriett John Plotts and his wife, Goldie Maude [Adams] Plotts, lived in Gordon. He was the Methodist Church minister in the 1950s. Their children were Charles Marriett Plotts and Marjorie Elizabeth Plotts. The Plotts' kept their granddaughters, Betsy and Sally while they were in Gordon, Ohio. Reverend and Mrs. Plotts are deceased. Betsy and Sally's parents were Howard Eugene Miller, born December 31, 1920 died April 18, 1987 and is buried at Rosehill Mausoleum in Springfield, Ohio. His wife, Marjorie Elizabeth [Plotts] Miller born May 14, 1922 is still living. Howard and Marjorie Miller had Sally Jo Miller, Elizabeth Ann Miller and Mark Kevin Miller. Sally married Richard Kenneth Shoaf on December 27, 1959 in Springfield, Ohio and had two daughters, Kimberly Robin Shoaf, and Daphne Shaun Shoaf. Kimberly married Jeffrey Buero and had two daughters, Katie Michelle and Sara Elizabeth.

Both born in Pompano Beacj, Florida and still reside there. Sally and Richard's youngest daughter, Daphne Shaun was married to Robert Minnick for 10 years and had a daughter, Ashley Elizabeth Minnick. Later they divorced and now she is married to Steven Johnston and they have a two year old son, Nathan Bradley. They live in Nashville, Tennessee. Both of Daphnes children were born in Tennessee - Ashley in Sevierville, and Nathan - Murfressboro. Betsy is married, and has a son and daughter and lives in Springfield, Ohio.

The Poe Family

Lafayette and Mary [Seibel] Poe lived in a home on Lot 32. Lafayette was a carpenter, by trade. Helen [Flory] Gentner remembers the family quite well because they lived across East Street from them. When Lafayette died and was buried at Ithaca Cemetery, Mary married Earlen "Earl" Idel whose first wife, Bertha, had died and was buried at Ithaca Cemetery. Grace [Idel] was Earl and Bertha's daughter as was Bertice. Bertice married (Leon's and Marcia's father whose name I have forgotten) and had the two children. Allen Poe died and was buried at Ithaca Cemetery at age 79 in 1952.

The Post Family

George Post was a native of New York, born December 29, 1809 and died on February 19, 1897. He moved from New York to Ohio in 1831 and lived near Hamilton, and Franklin. He married Martha [Rogers] Post, (born February 2, 1834 – died January 4, 1879) and had a son Ezra Post. He came to Gordon in 1839. He was one of the first members of the "Thomas Class" (Beginning of the Methodist Church in the area). Ezra Post owned the 36 acre farm west of Gordon. A "tile works and steam powered saw mill" were both located on his property in 1888. His wife, Mary, lived on the farm with George. The name is best known when associated with the Post Lumber Company in Gordon. Ezra Post also owned Lot 22 on Main Street in Gordon. In the 1880 Census, Martha

Black is a border at the Ezra Post home and is listed as a servant. The original farmhouse burned down on the Post farm. The farm was sold to William "Bill" Lage who had a home moved there from Lot 4 in the Post Addition on Railroad Street. Ezra and Mary and daughter, Grace moved into town in a new home built on Lot 9. Grace was still living there in 1910. She was a tailor. They had three sons, George B., Chester L., and Clifford W. Post (1900 Darke County Census). His brother, George B. Post, whose wife was named "Oleto", was an insurance agent in Gordon. They owned a number of acres south of the farm owned by, Ezra, and joining Joseph Eichelbarger's 7 acres. The Gordon Posts are deceased.

The Printz Family

David B. Printz, born May 28, 1932 in Dayton, the son of Mary [Boyer] Printz and Bill Printz has 5 brothers and 3 sisters. David B. Printz married Mary Beth [Younce] Printz, born December 5, 1933, the daughter of Mabel [Flory] Younce and Aubrey Younce. David and Mary Beth have four sons, Dale L. Printz, born February 5, 1953, Lonnie C. Printz, born February 13, 1956, Rodney N. Printz, born December 18, 1959 and Kyle D. Printz, born April 8, 1969. They moved to Gordon in December 1957 and lived on Bill and Ruth Lage's Farm, until March 1986. The farm was originally owned by Ezra Post.

The Rauscher Family

Charles Andrew Rauscher (born January 16, 1927) married Betty Jane [Fourman] Rauscher (born January 28, 1934).Charles and Betty had two daughters, Sheila Ann born May 13, 1957 and Melissa Marie born March 25, 1973. They had one son, Douglas Allen Rauscher born October 16, 1959. Sheila Ann lives in the country between Gordon and Verona, and Melissa Marie lives in Centerville (April 1989). Douglas is married to Jill Susan (Toops) Rauscher, born December 17, 1963. They had two children, Emily Michelle Rauscher born September 3, 1989 and Jessica

Lynn Rauscher born April 10, 1992.

The Reed Family

Joseph Reed, Company B, 110 Regiment OVI was born March 6, 1831 and died December 23, 1889 . He served in the Grand Army of the Republic. Marie P. Reed was born April 17, 1846 and died February 18, 1920 and is buried at Gordon Cemetery beside Joseph. Susan Reed died August 1, 1892 - age 67-1-8 and is buried at Gordon Cemetery. In 1910 a Joseph Reed, and his wife, Ida, lived on East Street. They had a son named Gerald. Hannah was a younger daughter in the photograph. Hannah [Reed] Cross is shown seated on a bench in front of the Blue Ribbon Creamery in a 1926 photo that I have. The 1910 Darke County, Ohio Census shows that Marie P. Reed, a 65 year old widow lived in Gordon with her two sons, Daniel E. Reed who was an electric railroad section hand and John Reed. Dan Reed and his wife Cora had a daughter, Marie. The family lived in Gordon. He was a (retired) farmer. Frank Reed was Dan's brother. Clara was Frank's wife's name. Frank died and was buried at Ithaca Cemetery at age 70 on November 15, 1947. Clara died and was buried at Ithaca Cemetery at age 74 on February 3, 1954. Wilbur O. Reed born August 4, 1907 died May 26, 1987 and his wife, Mary [Harleman] Reed died in February 1986.Both are buried at Ithaca Cemetery. They lived in Gordon on Lot 4 in Brown's Addition. Their children were Wilbur Reed Jr., died in the service during WW II, James W. Reed, Tom Reed, Glenn Dale Reed and Clara Joan [Reed] Toomey. Glenn Dale lives in Arcanum and Tommy Reed who now lives in Greenville, Ohio. Glenn's children are Debra Lynn [Reed] Stoneking of Franklin, Ohio, timothy Wayne Reed of Dayton, Jeffery Alan Reed of Lebanon, Ohio, Steven Douglas Reed of Germantown, and John Wilbur Reed of Mason, Ohio.

The Reichard Family

Isaac Reichard lived on Lot 20, on Main Street in 1857.

The Reinbarth Family

Frederick and his wife Bessie lived in Gordon, Frederick was a minister in 1900.

The Ressler Family

Lewis Manuel Ressler, born January 10, 1870, Mad River Township, Montgomery County, Ohio, died December 16, 1953, Harrison Township, Preble County, Ohio married Anna Mary [Smith] Ressler on September 12, 1889, at Verona, Ohio. He is buried at Verona Cemetery. His father and mother were John Henry Ressler and Anna Mary [Seigel] Ressler. Lewis Manuel's wife, Anna Mary [Smith] Ressler, was born July 9, 1867, Harrison Township, Preble County, Ohio and died there on August 14, 1960 at age 93 years 1 month and 5 days. Her father and mother were Jacob Smith and Sarah [Keltner] Smith. Lewis and Anna's children were; Jessie Marie Ressler, born April 4, 1890, died November 10, 1890, Lillie Leoto [Ressler] Fisher, born October 21, 1891, died February 20, 1981, married John Calvin Fisher. Myrtle May [Ressler] Moore born June 9, 1893, died January 15, 1951, married Orrean Harrison Moore. Milbert Evert Ressler, born January 29, 1895, died May 24, 1976, married Bonnie Marie [Bechtol] Ressler. Chester Berl Ressler, born December 12, 1896, died August 17, 1975, married Ruth Irene Fisher. Hazel [Ressler] Baker born March 24, 1899, died June 20, 1921, married Webster M. Baker, D. D. S.. Treva Sarah [Ressler] born January 23, 1903, she is deceased, married to Ozro Brown Hinea, and second married to S. DeWitt Baker. Berman Smith Ressler, born June 22, 1908, married Rhea Agnes Stout on September 4, 1935. Milbert Evert Ressler and Bonnie [Bechtol] Ressler lived just outside of Gordon on Gordon-Landis Road. They had Milbert Leon Ressler, born October 14, 1925, died October 14, 1925 and Harold "Dwight" Ressler born July 9, 1934 in Twin Township, Darke County, Ohio. Bonnie Marie [Bechtol] Ressler was born July 20, 1897 in Twin Township, Darke County, Ohio, and died February 9, 1972 at Eaton in Preble County, Ohio. Her parents were

William Bechtol and Idella "Della" [Troxell] Bechtol. Bonnie died and was buried at Ithaca Cemetery on February 12, 1972. She was 74. Milbert Ressler died and was buried at Ithaca Cemetery on May 27, 1976 at 81. Milbert Leon Ressler was stillborn in 1925.

The Rentfrow Family

John W. Rentfrow, John W. born in 1860 and died in1893 - age 37-10-14 and his wife Eliza J., born in 1870 and died in 1895 at age 24 were residents of Gordon and are buried at Gordon Cemetery.

The Rhodehamel Family

The Gordon Rhodehamels were natives of Shelby County, Ohio. They have a family plot in the cemetery in Pasco, Ohio. Nearly all of the Gordon Rhodehamels are buried at Ithaca Cemetery, Twin Township, Darke County, Ohio. William Allen "Bill" Rhodehamel, born August 30, 1897, and his first wife, Sarah, lived in a house on Lot 20 that was on the corner of Main and North Streets. Bill was a carpenter and worked for a number of years at the old Verona Lumber Yard, in Verona, Ohio. He also worked as a cabinetmaker out of a shop behind his house. Sarah chewed tobacco and smoked Kool cigarettes now and then, but in later years, Bill always denied that Sarah chewed or smoked. I can still see the tobacco juice running down the corners of her mouth. Vivia (my mother) and I were there, in their house, when Sarah died Cemetery, Bill yelled, "Sarah!" and leaped over the foot of the steel bed and landed on Sarah, crying hopelessly. Sarah, for a brief second, opened her eyes. Vivia told Bill not to do that, to let Sarah go in peace, and she did. Bill later married Vivia [Ballengee] Lincoln, and together had two children -- Charles Allen and Dorothy. Charles and Dorothy O'Dell live in Texas. Charles is married to Edna and it is Edna's second married. She brought one son, Frank, to their marriage. Dorothy married Denny McCloskey and divorced. She is married to an O'Dell at the present time. Vivia died January 4, 1998 at Wharton, Texas and is buried beside Bill at El Campo,

Texas at the Garden of Memories Cemetery (a long way from her "mommy" in West Virginia). Bill died on April 9, 1987 and is buried at El Campo, Texas at the Garden of Memories Cemetery. Bill's first wife, Sarah, is buried in Tennessee. Bill and Frank's father was, Charles Rhodehamel. Their mother was Gertrude [Dunlap] Rhodehamel. They lived near Sidney, Ohio. Bills brother, Frank, and his wife, Gertrude [Hosbrook] Rhodehamel, lived on North Street, in a house on Lot 6. Frank always drove a truck for a living. Their house was tiny but large enough to raise two strapping boys, Harold and Elmer Roscoe, who were by Frank's first wife, Grace Wiona [Batty] Rhodehamel. Both boys had lived in a "home" after their mother died. When Frank married Gertrude, the boys came to live with them. Harold recalled, in 1994, the big blizzard of 1936. He wrote, "I was going to school in Verona and they let us out early. It took us two and one-half hours to walk (22 to 3 miles) to Gordon and we were lucky to have made it. I froze both of my feet before we got home. Most of the kids rode the buses, but they had to stay at school." Elmer married Roberta Mae Mowry from Gordon and had two children. Mary Ann (still living in Union City, Indiana) and James Allen (deceased). Roberta died and was buried at Ithaca Cemetery on August 9, 1972 at age 47, and Elmer died June 13, 1972 and was buried at Ithaca Cemetery on June 17, 1974, age 52. James Allen, the son, died August 20, 1974 and was buried at Ithaca Cemetery on August 22, 1974 at age 22. All are buried at Ithaca Cemetery. Elmer worked for Dayton Tire and Rubber Company from 1950 until 1972 when he retired. Elmer was a veteran of World War II and served in the European and Pacific Theaters and was a member of the VFW, West Sonora Memorial 975 Post. He was a member of the Gordon Methodist Church and also a member of the Darke County Fish and Game Club. Harold lived in Greenville with his second wife, Betty [Fetters] Gordon and Betty's children, Butch, Susan and Cindy. He was a self-employed carpenter in later years. Harold died in 1997 and was buried at Ithaca Cemetery.

The Rice Family

William Rice is the owner of the home on Lot 19 in 1875. His wife was Mary J. They had sons, Harry C., a foreman; Clarence J., a railroad laborer, William D., a carpenter, and Edward B., a farmer. William S. Rice born married Ora Mae Tilman, (note spelling) daughter of Jacob and Lydia [Rhinehart] Tillman, on October 14, 1891. They had Hubert, born July 10, 1893 and Tillman P., born April 27, 1899. Ella Tillman, daughter of Henry and Permelia [House] Tillman, born 1831 in Preble County, Ohio, married John W. Rice. They had George, Levi, Jane, Dorothy and Arthur Rice. W. H. Rice is listed as having a shop on Main and Perry and was a blacksmith and a mechanic. They were also connected with hardware and lumber. His wife was, "Ethel Mae." This "William" died and was buried at Ithaca Cemetery in 1947 at age 77. Ethel died December 12, 1959 and is buried at Ithaca Cemetery. Harry Rice born in 1865 died in 1948 and was buried at Ithaca Cemetery at age 84 on October 14, 1948. His wife, Minnie, born in 1860 died in 1938 was buried at Ithaca Cemetery. Anna C. Rice was born in 1880 and died in 1958. She is buried at Ithaca Cemetery at age 79 on February 3, 1958. Edgar B. Rice, her husband, born in 1871 died in 1944 and is buried at Ithaca Cemetery. Helen [Flory] Gentner and Grace [Idel] Fisher both said the blacksmith shop was actually located on Lot 16 across Centre Street and they recall Charles "Tommy" Rice as being the blacksmith. The 1870 Darke County Ohio Census lists Henry as a blacksmith. His wife was Jane. They had four children, Charles, Mary, Clarence and Willie. Charles "Tommy" Rice was the blacksmith in the 1920s and both women remember him when they were small. I also remember Tommy Rice but his shop had moved to West Street. Charles "Tommy" Rice died and was buried at Ithaca Cemetery at age 80 on August 30, 1945. Charles married Sarah Ella Marcum, the sister of Charles Marcum of Gordon. They had one child, Ruth Rice who married William "Bill" Lage. The possibility is that the blacksmith shop was on Lot 17 and moved to 16 because it was later moved to West Street opposite Lot 24 on Main. The Warwick Hotel is still on Lot 15 on this map.

The Riffell Family

Robert Lowell Riffell, born January 27, 1934, at Delisle, Darke County, Ohio, the son of Harry Willis Riffell, born February 23, 1896 and Mary Olive [Marker] Riffell, born December 5, 1898, married October 13, 1951 Anna Louise [Ritz] Riffell, born April 11, 1936, the daughter of Raymond E. and Treva Elizabeth [Bruner] Ritz. Their children are Douglas Alan Riffell, born May 24, 1956, Lora Lee [Riffell] Rhodehamel, born May 14, 1952 and Vickie Elaine [Riffell] Edmonds, born November 22, 1953. The family live on North Street in Gordon, Ohio. Robert has one brother, John Mark Riffell, born March 11, 1926 and one sister, Helen Louise [Riffell] Neitzelt, born February 15, 1929. Lora Lee [Riffell] Rhodehamel married Michael E. Rhodehamel and had two children, Shane Edward Rhodehamel, born November 11, 1974, Jason Allen Rhodehamel, Born February 25, 1978, and Vickie Elaine [Riffell] Edmonds, born November 22, 1953, married Wayne Edmonds and had children Tracy Edmonds, Angie Edmonds and Ronnie Edmonds. Douglas Alan Riffell married December 21, 1978 Sharon [Brehm] Riffell and had children Gregory Riffell, born November 4, 1981, Monica Riffell, born May 28, 1984, and Emily Nicole Riffell born November 25, 1987.

The Robbins Family

Albert S. "Al Robbins was born in 1864. He lived with his wife, Mary, on Gordon - Landis Road. He loafed either at the coal office and the blacksmith shop or on the bench in front of Pinkerton's store. Al died and was buried at Ithaca Cemetery on February 6, 1943 at age 68. Mary died and was buried at Ithaca Cemetery on August 2, 1940 at age 79. Amy Robbins died and was buried at Ithaca Cemetery at age 79 on July 20, 1926.

The Robinson Family

Loren and Ethel Robinson lived in Gordon in the house on North Street that was once owned by Charley Shepherd. They had four sons, Paul, Ronnie, James and Gary. Paul married Marilyn Black who lived across the street.

The Rogers Family

Clarence Rogers and his mother, Rozenna Rogers, lived in a house on Lot 33 at the time Helen [Flory] Rogers and Clarence Rogers were married. Clarence and his mother had moved to Gordon after Clarence's father died. Clarence died of a tumor on the spine and complications therefrom on March 8, 1944. He was 46. He is buried in Ithaca Cemetery. Helen [Flory] Rogers, born July 16, 1912, and Clarence E. Rogers, born in October 7, 1898, had one son, Allen E. Rogers, born January 5, 1939 at Gordon, Ohio. Allen had three half-sisters, Pearl [Rogers] McGraw, Ruth [Rogers] Naseman, and Francis [Rogers] Stansberry. Allen E. Rogers married Nova L. [Rhoades] Rogers the daughter of Dorothy K. [Bashore] Rhoades and Ivan E. Rhoades, from Darke County, Gettysburg, Ohio in 1960. They have two daughters, Durinda [Rogers] Simmerman and Shelly Kay [Rogers] Lane. Durinda married Harold Simmerman and they had one son, Jeffrey P. Simmerman. Harold had one son, Bradley Thomas Canan. Shelly married William C. Lane Jr., and they had three children. Steven C., Brandon A. and Sharayah J. Lane. Allen and Nova live in West Milton, Ohio.

The Rurode Family

Ralph E. Rurode was born September 17, 1936 and his wife, Linda S. [Newman] Rurode, was born September 25, 1941. They live in Gordon, Ohio on Centre Street. Ralph's parents were Charles Jacob Rurode (deceased) born February 22, 1893, and Ada May Rurode (deceased) born November 11, 1895. Ralph has one brother, Robert D. Rurode, born April 29, 1933 and Sisters, Mary [Rurode] Boone, born December 19, 1923, and Catherine [Rurode] Lavy born February 15, 1929, and Sophia [Rurode] Simmons (deceased) born March 29, 1925, and Martha [Rurode] Sides (deceased) born April 23, 1920. Linda S. [Newman] Rurode's parents were Ethel May Newman and Emory E. Newman (deceased). George and Clarence Weimer lived in the same house in the 30s and 1940s.

The Schaar Family

Robert E. "Bob" Schaar, born March 10, 1933 and his wife Rozenna [Shelton] Schaar, born March 6, 1941, lived in Gordon, at 504 North St. They have two children, Randy E. and Bonnie Marie. They live in Port Charlotte, Florida.

The Scheiding Family

George Scheiding lived across from the grocery store and post office with Charles and Carrie Miller and Margaret Henninger lived there. Jay Scheiding (no relation to George that I know) is married and lives in Florida. He went to Gordon School. Albert H. Scheiding, born 1865, died 1867, Charles A., born 1879, died 1871, and Louis J., born 1880 and died 1880 are buried in Gordon Cemetery. Margaret, wife of John Scheiding, was born in 1837, and died in 1880 is buried in Gordon Cemetery.

The Schlechty Family

Samuel Schlechty, born in 1830, died in 1905 and his wife, Catharine Schlechty, born 1853, lived in Gordon. Catharine lived in the south end of Gordon, in 1900 (census) age 56, and was still living there in 1910 (Gordon Directory). She was a widow. A niece, Laura A. Redmon, age

28, was living with her in 1910 (census). Samuel and Catharine are buried at Ithaca Cemetery.

The Schnorf Family

John Schnorf, died February 25, 1863 - age 25-2-15. Joseph died August 1, 1882 - age 71-8-18. Sarah died April 5, 1894 - age 84-1-29. All are buried at Gordon Cemetery.

The Schwartz Family

Herbert M. Schwartz, born November 25, 1909 and his wife Anna, born July 17, 1912, had a six children. They moved into the Ed Ammon store building after the Gunder family left town. Their children were, Robert, Richard, Jeanette, Wilda Ann, Patricia and Mary Lou. Robert Schwartz, born July 15, 1930,lives with his wife, Jean, in Florida. They live in Venice, Florida. Bob has two sons, Robert and Rodney, and two daughters, Deborah K and Kimberly, by his first marriage. Richard D. Schwartz, born August 18, 1933, married Marilyn Schwartz and lives in Piqua, Ohio. They have four children, Richard D. Jr., Wendy R., Keith A., and Kelly Jo. Jeanette A. Schwartz, born September 16, 1931, married Charles Wick and lives in West Alexander, Ohio. They have three children, Jerry L., James E., and Daniel W. Wick. Wilda Ann Schwartz, born July 3, 1935, married George Snyder in 1953 and moved to Phillipsburg, Ohio. They have four boys, Timothy A., Gale G., Kevin B., and Rory T. Pat Schwartz, born July 6, 1938, married George Tucker, Jr. They live near Brookville, Ohio. They have two children and four grandchildren. Steven E., and Cathy L. [Tucker] Smith. Mary Lou Schwartz was born January 26, 1949. She has two children, Kurtis and James J. Hemmerick. The family lives in Lewisburg, Ohio.

The Selby Family

Jacob Selby and his Wife, Alice Selby lived in Gordon in 1936 on East Street.

The Sensenbaugh Family

Russell H. Sensenbaugh, born October 28, 1894 died on October 8, 1978 is buried at Ithaca Cemetery. His wife, Cora J. [Pyles] Sensenbaugh, born August 6, 1895, died July 22, 1954, is also buried at Ithaca Cemetery. They had two daughters, June and Janice. June married Bob Olwine in 1947. They had one son, Gregory. June retired to West Palm Beach, Florida. She died February 14, 1998. Janice married Robert "Bob" Beaver. They had two sons, Robert Scott and Steven. They have four grandchildren. Bob Beaver is deceased. Robert Scott married Sherri [Baker] Beaver. They live in Palm Beach Gardens, Florida and have no children. Steven B. Beaver married Tracy [Heisy] Beaver and they have four children, Mandi, Angela, Shawn and Jeremy. They live in Ansonia, Ohio.

The Shahan Family

Most people who lived in Gordon, in the 1930s and 1940s will remember "Dovie" Shahan. I have several photographs of her, but have not found any record of her family. She was there and went to school in Gordon, and that's all I know or can find out. I do know she is deceased, but lest her name be lost to history, I have included it here.

The Shank Family

Hobart and Esther Shank lived in Gordon on Lot 42 in the 1950s. Their children were Ronnie, Robert "Buddy" and Karen Shank. Bobbie still lives in the same house with his wife Sue (1998).

The Sharp Family

Joseph Sharp and his wife, Julia lived in Gordon when the 1870 census was taken. He is listed as working in the shoe shop.

The Shepard Family

James Alvin Shepard and Nancy Catherine [Stover] "Cassie" Shepard lived with their children Grace M., Oscar, Hazel, Robert C., Author L. (Arthur?), and Mamie M. on the far south end of town. Sarah A. Shepard, widow, 72, lived in the same household. James and Nancy lived in a log house in the woods just west of town where the Price Family lived, or, earlier the farm belonged to Bill Lage in the early 1900s. They moved north of Gordon on the farm on the west side of the road that would belong to the Wick Family and lived there until 1918, and then moved east of town to the farm across State Route 722 from where Marvin Miller lives today. They bought the house on Lot 3 in Brown's Addition during WW II and in 1949 sold it to Wilbur and Mary Reed. Oscar Ora Shepard, born 1899, died 1969 the son of James Alvin Shepard and Nancy Catherine [Stover] Shepard, and Mildred Ilo [Peden] Shepard, born 1903, died 1994 the daughter of George Everett Peden and Grace E. [Combs] Peden, lived on Lot 26 when I knew them, and had four children. Roger Allen Shepard, born December 11, 1928 in the house on Lot 5 on Railroad Street, died June 3, 1981, married Betty Jane [Harleman} Shepard July 22, 1950 (see Harleman for their children). James Arthur "Jimmy" Shepard, born April 30, 1931, married Joan Fuller on June 19, 1954. Their children are Theresa Ann [Shepard] Kelly, born June 20, 1955, married Bruce Dale Kelly. James David Shepard, born April 14, 1956. Mark Stephen Shepard, born February 23, 1957, died February 25, 1957. Thomas Gerard Shepard, Born January 20, 1959, died January 21, 1959. Kathleen Marie [Shepard] Pewitt born March 17, 1961, married February 23, 1985 James Richard Pewitt. And Jean marie Shepard, born August 27, 1964. William Cecil "Bill" Shepard, born September 24, 1932, married April 17, 1957 Rosalyn Jean [Williams]

Shepard, born September 25, 1935. Their children are Beth E. [Shepard] Studebaker, born January 26, 1958, married December 19, 1988 Dr. John Studebaker (second spouse). David Earl Shepard, born July 8, 1961. And Stephen Edward Shepard, born July 11, 1967 married Stephanie. Carol Joyce [Shepard] Ritz, born April 27, 1935, married January 17, 1958 Larry Wayne Ritz. Their children are Sheryll Ann [Ritz] Wetzel, born March 28, 1960, married January 17, 1998 David Wetzel. Peggy Sue [Ritz] Dill, born March 18, 1964, married July 25, 1987 Patrick Dill. And Melinda Louise [Ritz] Kauffman, born December 4, 1971, married September 19, 1992 Timothy Kauffman (see Kauffman). Oscar was a metal finisher at Frigidaire Division of G. M. C. in Dayton. Oscar was buried at Ithaca Cemetery. Mildred Shepard was buried at Ithaca Cemetery on June 4, 1994. She was 89.

The Shepherd Family

Charles M. "Charley" Shepherd lived in the last house on North Street heading west toward Ithaca in 1936. The lot was one acre, narrow and deep. George and Ella Eller lived there around 1910 and Jack Kronenberg and his family lived in the same house in the late 1940s. Charles' wife's name was Alice Shepherd. They ran a small garage there and sold gasoline. It is listed as a "Filling Station."

The Shillingburg Family

The Shillingburg family lived on a small farm across the road and west of the Gordon school house. Ora A. Shillinburg, born August 20, 1880, died November 4, 1957, and was buried at Ithaca Cemetery. Cena D. Shillingburg born April 2, 1880, died on April 15, 1942, and was buried at Ithaca Cemetery at age 61 on April 18, 1942. Eli Shillingburg and his wife Neva had two children, Robert and Kathleen. Robert married Marjorie in 1946 and they had two children. Lee of Kettering and daughter, Cena of Huber Heights. Cena was probably named after her Grandmother, Cena. Robert lives in Arcanum, Ohio. Kathleen married a man whose name is

Strock. She is deceased at age 79. Buried at Ithaca Cemetery.

The Shoenfelt Family

Emma Shoenfelt lived next door to us. She was the midwife who was there with my mother the day I was born (October 25, 1934). The Shoenfelt house was on Lot 4 of the "Post Addition" on Railroad Street. The house was sold and moved to replace the home burned on the Post farm. Mary Post lived on the farm immediately behind us. After the house burned, the farm was sold. Bill Lage bought the farm from Mary Post and he also bought the Shoenfelt home and had it moved across the field and put it on a new foundation. It still stands and is the farm house most people recognize as belonging to the farm. My father bought the empty lot after the house was moved and Pat and I lived in the Blacksmith Shop (house) that was moved there in the late 1940s.

The Silver Family

The 1910 Darke County Ohio Census records the name with an "s." None of the maps show this, but rather show "Silver." Horatio Z. Silver was a physician in Gordon on the same lot as Dr. Van Pelt. His wife's name was Louisa and they had a daughter, Helen Silver. In 1920 she was 8. Dr. Silver also had a servant, Lora Smith living with them in 1900.

The Sims Family

Sam and Georgia Sims lived on Railroad Street on Lot 4. They are deceased and buried at Ithaca Cemetery. They lived in the house (Tommy Rice's blacksmith shop) that Pat and I had lived in for several years.

The Sluterbeck Family

The Charles Sluterbeck family lived just south of Gordon on a farm. Their house was one of the most beautiful farm houses in the area (according to Helen [Flory] Gentner who saw it in the 1920s), and it was still a wonderful place when I grew up there in the 1940s. It has since been allowed to fall into disrepair and any hope of restoring it is out of the question. Charles Sluterbeck's wife was named Cary, and they had a daughter, Cecil. Charles Sluterbeck died and was buried at Ithaca Cemetery at age 69 on March 23, 1955.

The Small Family

Robert Small and his wife, Ethel, lived on Railroad Street in Gordon, Ohio and are listed as residents in the Darke County Directory - Directory of Gordon, Ohio.

The Smith Family

Roy C. Smith, born November 11, 1899 and his wife, Frances K. [Emerick] Smith, born February 11, 1913 lived on Gordon Landis Road. Their children are Betty Joan [Smith] Eckman, born April 2, 1934 at Hartle Road, Ansonia, Ohio, and Titia Rose [Smith] Holmes, born September 30, 1937 at Elijah-York Road, Ansonia, Ohio, and Jimmy D. Smith, born October 12, 1944. Titia Rose married William L. Holmes Sr., born November 1, 1936. His parents are Irene [Eubank] Holmes and Halford H. Holmes. Betty Joan married Francis S. "Andy" Eckman, born December 28, 1930. His parents are Olive Withney [Westfall] Eckman and Lester George Eckman.

Carl E. Smith and his wife, Wilma, and son, Wayne lived on East Street on Lot 40. He was a clerk at the Bowser Grocery Store.

The Schnorf Family

The J. Schnorf family lived on Lots 24 and 25 on both sides of Centre Streets in 1857.

The Snyder Family

Peter Snyder died April 20, 1862 - age 73-5-14 and is buried at Gordon Cemetery. Robert Harold Snyder (b. April 25, 1905, d. April 10, 1988) and his wife, Treva [Schaar] Snyder (b. July 29, 1903, d. December 24, 1980) lived on Gordon-Landis Road. Their small farm adjoins the western boundary of Gordon. The family moved to Gordon in 1948 and lived there until Gordon school closed in 1951. The Snyder family then moved to Arcanum. Fred Snyder is deceased. Betty Snyder has been crippled by Polio and was in a wheelchair when the family lived in Gordon. After the family moved to Arcanum, Betty married a man by the name of Phillips and had a daughter. Betty now lives with her daughter in Waynesville, Ohio. Grace Snyder married a man by the name of Bard. They moved to Sandusky, Ohio. Alice Snyder married Charles Hiser and moved to Ludlow Falls. Ohio. They have a son, Steven Charles Hiser, who was born in 1967 and their daughter, Nancy Kay Hiser, was born in 1962. Douglas Snyder married Margaret Ann Lengerich. They have two children, Derrick and Tonya and live in Piqua, Ohio. Donald Snyder is married and lives in Sidney, Ohio.

The Stephens Family

Ted Howard Stephens, born June 23, 1951, in Dayton, Ohio, and wife, Rebecca Lynne (Houdeshell) "Becky" Stephens, born June 23, 1951 moved to Gordon, Ohio in 1974. Their children, Matthew H., born January 21, 1974, and Michael A., born January 21, 1974 and Jonathan W. Stephens, born May 3, 1976 live on Scott Street. Matthew Stephens married Kati [Miller] Stephens on August 13, 1995 and built a new home on Scott Street. Ted H. Stephens' parents are Wilma Stephens, born April

8, 1929 and Leonard Stephens, born May 13, 1928. Ted's brothers are Doug Stephens, born November 29, 1948, and Bruce E. Stephens, born March 6, 1950. His sister is Kay Jane Stephens, born September 29, 1954. Rebecca's parents are Ava A. Houdeshell and Burldean F. Houdeshell (deceased).

The Stewart Family

George F. Stewart, and Florence L. [Joliff] Stewart and their children, Harold "Bill", Jack, Don, George, Robert, Mary and Karen lived on Scott and East Streets (Lot 32). Harold "Bill" Stewart, born October 12, 1932 married Barbara [Myers] Stewart, born October 8, 1939 and they had William "Bill" Jr., Cathy Lynn, Jimmy Earl, Larry Eugene and Rebecca Ann. Bill and his family moved away from Gordon to Piqua. He served a hitch in the Army as a front line medic during the Korean War. He lives in Conover, Ohio.

The Stine Family

The Stine family lived in Gordon in the south end. The mother's name is Verna Stine. The children and who they married are Billy S. Stine. Billy married Evelyn Van Zant. They had three daughters. The family now lives in Sidney, Ohio. Lee W. Stine married Jean Boatman. They had five children. Jean passed away in 1983 at age 52. The family lives in Huber Heights, Ohio. David W. Stine married Pegge Green from West Milton. They have four children. They live in Ludlow Falls, Ohio. Barbara Stine married Charles Hampton. They have four children and live in Troy, Ohio. Darlene Stine married Billy Hall from Frederick. They have four children and live at Ludlow Falls, Ohio. Kathy Stine married Delmar Elifritz. They have six children and live in Bradford, Ohio.

The Stonerock Family

Thomas Cleveland Stonerock was the son of Jonathan B. and Margaret Ann [Wissinger] Stonerock. His father was a Civil War veteran having served in Company E. 40th O. V. I. And Company E., 51st O. V. I. Thomas was born May 1884 in Patterson Township of Darke County, Ohio. His paternal grandparents were Samuel and Catherine [Metzger] Stonerock who arrived in Darke County, Ohio on or before 1830 from Greene County, Ohio. His maternal grandfather was William Wissinger who came from Virginia and settled in Darke County. On March 4, 1905, Thomas Married Susan "Susie" Catherine [Neff] in Darke County. Susan was the daughter of Perry W. and Catherine [Landers] [Neff] Stonerock. To this couple were born three children: Lawrence W. Stonerock, Charles E. Stonerock and Goldie P. [Stonerock] Stultz. Thomas was an ambitious grocer who owned three grocery stores, in Hillgrove, Palestine and Gordon, Ohio. His store in Hillgrove suffered a disastrous fire in 1923, which not only wiped out the store, but the family residence as well. The store he owned and operated in Gordon was the Charles "Mont" Mundhenk store and William and Lillian Boyer owned and operated it after Stonerock. A 1936 Darke County, Ohio, Twin Township Directory for 1936 shows Tom Stonerock as the owner of the store. Thomas died in 1949 in Dayton, Ohio. Susie died February 15, 1953 in Greenville, Ohio. Both were members of the Happy Corner Church of the Brethren near Clayton, Ohio, and are buried in the Abbottsville Cemetery.

The Strobel Family

Andrew G. Strobel, died April 22, 1881 - age 67-2-22 and his wife, Lilly, born Montgomery County, Ohio, March 17, 1822 died March 23, 1876 - age 54 years 6 days. Levi son of A. G. & Delilah died December 5, 1860 - age 1 month 12 days. Mary E. daughter of A. G. and D. died May 1, 1860 - age 1-1-26. Infant daughter died October 9, 1858. John W. son of A. & L. died July 31, 1874 - Age 22-1-7. All are buried at Gordon Cemetery.

The Studebaker Family

Alice S. Studebaker was living in Gordon on Perry Street in 1910 (Gordon Directory).Mrs. Studebaker is the teacher shown in the Big Room in 1904 in a Gordon School photograph. She is also shown, but not identified, in a 1911 school photograph of both rooms, taken outside. The Small Room had a male teacher. (see Feitshans).

The Stump Family

John Harvey Stump born in 1900 died 1967, and his 1st wife, Martha Jeanette [Grubbs] Stump had a son, Junior Marlene Stump. Junior married Betty June Stump and had Sandra Jeanne [Stump] Stutz who married John Wesley Stutz and they had a son, Mark Allen Stutz born in 1967. Cynthia Lea [Stump] Leffew married Jerry Dale Leffew and they had William John Leffew in 1970 and Todd Anthony Leffew in 1973. Steven John Stump married Patty [Ernst] Stump and had Steven John Stump Junior in 1978. Stanley L. Stump born in 1949 married Susan Elaine [Kamm] Stump and they had Douglas Scot Stump in 1970 and Staci Renae Stump in 1973. Cheryl Ann Stump born in 1954 married Mary Dwayne Coss. She also married Jimmie Ray Brummerstedt and they had Kendra Nicole Brummerstedt in 1980. Junior Stump died and was buried at Ithaca Cemetery at age 57 on April 17, 1982. John's 2nd wife, Erma [Folck] Kronenberg, Stump born January 11, 1914 died March 1965, also had two children, Michael Gene Stump, born in 1951 and Debra Mae Stump born in 1953. Janet Kronenberg, Erma's child by her first marriage is deceased as is her son Edward "Ed." Jack Kronenberg is alive and living in California. Michael Gene Stump married Patricia Kay [Sharp] Stump born in 1955. They had two children, Stephanie Lynne Stump born in 1976 and John Calvin Stump born in 1980. Debra Mae [Stump] married Jan Snyder born in 1951 and they had two children, Teri Snyder and Kevin John Snyder. Michael and his family are the owners of the Philip and Elizabeth Gordon homestead that his grandfather, John owned. John Stump born in 1900 and his wife, Martha born 1904 died 1948 also called "Erma," had two children, Janet and John Junior. John Junior got married and had one son, Mike.

The Sturgell Family

John T. Sturgell, born September 14, 1952 and his wife, Janice [Burchfield] Sturgell, born November 14, 1955 have lived in Gordon, Ohio for eighteen years (1998) on East Street. Janice's mother is Neva [Howdishell] Burchfield, born November 14, 1925 and her father is Issia Vaughan Burchfield, born June 3, 1917. Janice has three brothers, David, born December 28, 1950, Ronald, born November 23, 1952 and Gary, born February 25, 1965. John T. Sturgell's father is Ivan Bert Sturgell and his mother is Aliene Sturgell.

The Sullivan Family

James G. Sullivan, born March 13, 1916, died July 12, 1985, and his wife, Dorothy LaVerne [McCracken] Sullivan, born July 20, 1920 lived in Gordon, Ohio with their children on Lot 24 on Main Street. The children are Judith M. [Sullivan] Ery, born July 28, 1942, in Columbus, Ohio, and Jeanne [Sullivan] Kepler, born May 18, 1938, and James G. Sullivan, Jr., born October 10, 1943, and Joseph L. Sullivan, born April 27, 1945. Second marriage for Dorothy LaVerne Sullivan to Clarence Loessberg in 1989.

The Thacker Family

The Gordon Postmaster for a number of years was Jerry Thacker. He and his wife, Catherine, "Kathy" operated the post office in town.

The Thompson Family

Hildebert J. Thompson and his wife, Katie, lived in Gordon, Ohio with their son Charles W. in 1910 (census).

The Thorp Family

William Thorp lived in Gordon with his wife, Helen, on Lot 49. He was a laborer (1870 Darke County, Ohio Census). His children were, Mary E. Thorp, Florence 14, Kate, 12, Jennett, 9, Susan, 5, Charles, 2 months. Five years later, 1875 , on a map of Gordon, the father, William, is still living at the same location. Mary Thorp lived on Lot 5 and 6 in a home facing Centre Street. She was 77 and Florence 14 lived with her in the 1870 Darke County, Ohio census.

The Tice Family

William Tice lived in Gordon with his wife, Lucy A. Tice. He worked in the hotel and it appears, from the 1870 Darke County Census that he owns it - "hotel keeper" is the listing. An 1875 map of Gordon shows a building on Main Street listed as "Gordon Town Hotel." The Tice family had two children, Ella and Bubby.

The Townsend Family

Most people are surprised to learn that Gordon was the home of the "Ohio Pure Food Company" (see that listing for more information). The Townsend family owned it. Susan Townsend, owned 4 acres of ground along North Street and at the head of East Street on a 1910 map. In the 1920s and 1930s, daughters Ella and Emma lived together in a home on Lot 9 on Perry Street. Emma was never married but did have a son, Merrill (Merle?). He worked as a bookkeeper for his mother in the family business and in the post office. Emma, her son, and sister, Ella Mae Townsend lived in a home on Perry Street on Lot 9. The other sister was Pearl Townsend. Pearl was a singer and a teacher. She was seldom in Gordon because her singing career kept her in several larger cities. She was an opera singer. The post office was awarded to a Republican when they won the elections and to a Democrat when they won. The Townsends ran the post office from their home on Perry Street.

The Troxel Family

David Troxel and his wife, Mary Ann, born January 12, 1835, died April 30, 1917 and daughter, Hetta, and sons, Watson and John D. lived in Gordon in 1880 with Ann Marshall, a widow. They kept one border, John Rouge who was a laborer. Mary Ann Troxel lived in Gordon and was listed in the 1900 Darke County, Ohio Census as a "capitalist" and her mother, Anna Marshall, a widow, who lived with her died December 12, 1881 - age 16-3-7. Watson E. son of D. & Mary A. The Family are buried at Gordon Cemetery.

The Troutman Family

Rebecca Troutman lived on a lot north of Lot 29. She is shown on two maps - 1875 and 1888. She was not there in 1910.

The Trump Family

Nora Trump lived in house on split Lot 30. Oscar and Mildred Shepard were her neighbors to the north and the Mowry family were neighbors to the south. Jack Foland Jr., and his wife, Rhonda [Moore] Foland, presently own the home.

The Van Pelt Family

Dr. George P. and his wife Ella lived on the corner of Main and North Streets on Lot 21. The house had also been the home of Drs. Overholser and Silver. Dr. Van Pelt delivered most of the babies born in Gordon from the time he moved there until he left town. They had one son, Gerald Van Pelt. Gerald married Estelle and lives in New Orleans, Louisiana. Gerald and his wife had two daughters -- Virginia and Margaret. When Gerald Van Pelt went to school in Gordon, he says he went there in the 6th, 7th and 8th grades and Mr. Studebaker was his teacher. Gerald, who now lives in New Orleans, Louisiana.

The Warwick (Worwick) Family

In 1857, Weston Warwick owned and operated the hotel in Gordon. The hotel was situated on Lot 15. William Warwick, (This name is spelled Worwick on some tombstones and Warwick on others) born in 1878 died in 1951 married Maude Mae Warwick born in 1875 died in 1930. Maude was buried at Ithaca Cemetery on March 25, 1930 at the age of 54. Mary Warwick died and was buried at Ithaca Cemetery on March 19, 1936 at age 92. She was 13 when her family's hotel was listed on the 1857 Gordon map. John and Mary Warwick lived in Gordon in 1870. They had two sons, Delano, 2 years old, and Daniel 14 months. Delano Warwick was born in 1867 and died in 1860 and was buried at Ithaca Cemetery on February 10, 1960 at age 92. Elizabeth A. Warwick died and was buried at Ithaca Cemetery on August 15, 1961 at age 93. In 1875, F. M. Warwick owned two triangular shaped lots beside the railroad tracks in Gordon. The 1870 Darke County Census shows a Francis Warwick and his wife, Margaret. He was a day laborer.

The Weimer Family

George and Clarence Weimer lived on Centre Street and for a while their sister Amanda "Mandy" lived there with them. George Weimer died and was buried at Ithaca Cemetery at age 88 on April 14, 1950. Their brother, Charles "Charley" Weimer lived alone on East Street. All of the Weimers are buried at Ithaca Cemetery.

The Weisenbarger Family

The Townsend sisters' home became the home of John and Ollie Weisenbarger who lived there with their son, Dean Weisenbarger. Russell Weisenbarger and his wife, Gladys, lived in a home on Lot 5. They had two boys, John and Jerry. John married Nancy Fourman and had two children, Melissa and Steven. They live in Arcanum. Jerry Weisenbarger never married. He is retired from General Motors and lives at the east edge of Gordon on State Route 722. Russell worked at Carpentry at Frigidaire, Division of General Motors. Elmer Weisenbarger was the Sunday School Superintendent for 33 years at the Gordon Methodist Church. His son, Hubert, took on that responsibility in later years. Hubert, Elmer's son, married "Mildred" and had one daughter, Sherry. They bought the Doctors Overholser, Silver and Van Pelt residence on Lot 21 in 1945 and moved in in 1957. Their daughter, Sherry, was born there. Sherry is married and her husband is a District Judge in Muskegon, Michigan. They have four children. Hubert was a lathe operator at the Dayton Rubber Manufacturing Company (1949). Naomi Weisenbarger married Lowell Landis, a school teacher. They had four children. Richard Weisenbarger graduated from Monroe High School in 1949 and was married in 1953. They had three children, Kay, Kevin and Christen. They live in Melbourne, Florida. There is a Jacob and Barbara Weisenbarger listed on the 1850 census of Twin Township

The Whiting Family

Donald E. Whiting, born October 23, 1922 in Dayton, Ohio and his wife, Ruby E. [Brown] Whiting, born October 10, 1925 (now deceased) live in Gordon, Ohio. They live in the Levi Ammon house situated on the 1_ acre site across from Andrew Gordon's original home on Lot 30. Donald Whiting's mother, Esther J. [Nash] Whiting was born September 29, 1904 and his father, Edwin E. Whiting was born September 18, 1895. Ruby's mother is Mary E. [Fourman] Brown and her father is Donald J. Brown. Donald and Ruby have four children. Donald E. Whiting, born May 18, 1946, and Nelda K. [Whiting] Morris, born August 19, 1947, and Ronald E. Whiting, born December 13, 1949 and John R. Whiting, born

January 9, 1954.

The Wick Family

Charles Wick married Jeanette Schwartz. Frigidaire, a Division of General Motors, employed Charles, a plumber, as a punch press operator. They had one son, Jerry. Albert Lowell Wick (Charles' brother) is married. They had a number of children while living in Gordon, Ohio, but now live on State Route 49, Arcanum.

The Wilker Family

Annie Wilker lived on Main Street in Gordon in 1936. She is listed in the Darke County Directory for that year as a resident of Gordon, Ohio.

The Winters Family

Gene and Marcella Winters lived on Railroad Street on Lot 4. They had two children.

The Woodbury Family

Lyman and Mabel Woodbury lived for a time on Main Street on Lot 18. They had one daughter, Helen. They ran the Gordon Post Office out of their home for a number of years. Helen married Robert "Bob" Klink. They had two daughters. Helen was killed in an auto accident at the intersection of SR 722 and Gordon-Landis Road.

The Wright Family

Robert V. Wright and his wife, Juanitta, lived on North Street on the original _ acre lot on the south side of the street adjoining West Street. Their children are Reggie, Gary, Shirley Charlene, Diana, and Ronnie. Reggie recently died (1997-98).

The Yantis Family

Jeff and Julie Yantis and their children live in Gordon in the house once owned by Dr. Van Pelt on Lot 21 (1998).

The Zeller Family

Benjamin 25 and Emily Zeller 26 lived in Gordon, Ohio with their son, Henry. Benjamin was a saddle maker.

The Zimmerman Family

The Zimmerman family lived in Gordon on Lot 7. Mr. Zimmerman was dead and Lena Zimmerman was a widow at age 39 when the census was taken. Her children were Paul, Bernice who married a Leon Fisher's father, Charles, Gladis who married a Blower and Esther (Also spelled Ester) who married a Reford Cawood. Reford and Esther had two children, Carl, a minister in North Manchester, Indiana, and Barbara, a nurse in Yelm, Washington. Lena Zimmerman was a sister to the Weimer brothers who were all bachelors and lived in Gordon.

Gordon Cemetery (read from inscriptions)

Roberts, George A. born March 14, 1852 - died January 14, 1886

Barnhart, Lena L. and Charles A. - no dates on either

Rentfrow, John W. 1860-1893 - age 37-10-14 (Father)

Eliza J. (his wife) 1870-1895 - age 24-8-21 [24 years, 8 months and 21 days] (Mother)

Barklow, Samuel born July 25, 1851 died January 4, 1920

Ellenora born February 22, 1852 - died December 30, 1945

Laura Hendrick born September 25, 1816, died May 31, 1895 - age 78-8-6.

Elizabeth born January 3, 1814 died December 23, 1903 - age 89-11-20 side/side.

Corzatt, Guy (1878-1938 - Addie 1883-19__ (Fresh Grave when read) (It was his wife)

Gift, William (Wm) H. Company E, 87 Ohio Infantry 1839-1913 (G.A.R.)

E. E. 1843-1921 (Mother)

Black, Cleo B. died June 15, 1905 - age 1 month

Andrew died April 14, 1896 - age 46-9-27

Lanie wife of Andrew died June 9, 1892 - age 37-4-29

Ola M. daughter of Andrew and Lanie died September 15, 1890 - age 1-3-22

Ova O. daughter of Andrew and Lanie died July 6, 1892 - age 3 months - s/s

Joseph died March 31, 1891 - age 67-3-18 (Father)

Susanna died April 19, 1894 - age 81-5-2 (Mother) s/s

Marshall, Anna M. born December 2, 1813, died March 13, 1907 s/s Mary Troxal

Troxal, Mary A. born January 12, 1835, died April 30, 1917 s/s Anna M. Marshall

Watson E. son of D. & Mary A. died December 12, 1881 - age 16-3-7

Black, Cora E. daughter of A. & L. died October 7, 1892 - age 12-1-16 s/s as Blacks above

Bolinger, Horatio S. died September 2, 1893 - age 25-3-1

Letta M. died April 14, 1891 - age 20-4-3. Infant born April 7, 1891 s/s

Mundhenk, Cora A. daughter of William (Wm) and Minerva E. died Sep. 30, 1879 - age 3-5-3

Minerva E. wife of William A. died November 11, 1887 - age 34-7-1

Bolinger, Lawrence W. son of DB and L.P. born February 22, 1909 died July 26, 1909

M. Bolinger died August 28, 1900 - age 83-5-11 (Father)

Annie G. (Wife) died August 6, 1890 - age 66-6-18 s/s

Albright, Allen 1830-1899 - Elizabeth (Wife) 1828-1887 s/s Allen G. A. R.

Wolf, Francis Edward son of John and Matilda died October 20, 1880 - age 4?y 10m d?

Warwick, F. M. born December 1, 1848 died May 10, 1882 G. A. R.

Margaret C. born December 10, 1851 died January 1, 1935

Sarah born November 9, 1870 died August 14, 1871 s/s

Kitt, Bryan died July 11, 1881 - age 54 years

Eichelbarger, John died August 2, 1906 - age 67-5-23 - Co. A 152

Regiment ONC G. A. R.

_____? Etta daughter of J. & M. J. died March 12, 1873 - age 2 years 18 days

Marie J. wife of John died August 28, 1879 - age 21 10 11

Corzatt, George H. Company C, 4 Ohio Cavalry G. A. R.

Scheiding, Fredericks L. 1871-1886

_____Infant Born and died April 3, 1888 no last name given

Thorp, William (Wm) T. 1827-1889 - Ella (Wife) s/s

Infant son of Wm. T. and Ella died January 27, 1871

Verbryhe, Laurence died March 23, 1876 - age 53-5-18

Clark, Emma J. daughter of J. M. & M. H. died August 9, 1873 - age 2 years

Cosler, Caroline M. died November 6, 1889 - age 67-10-12 (Mother)

Graham, William born in Ireland December 3, 1803 died December 1, 1882 - age 73-11-28

Hipple, Henry 1813-1894 - Elizabeth F. 1825-1891 s/s

Mary A. 1847-1930 (Mother)

Rosmeier, Anna M. wife of G. born July 27, 1821 died November 17, 1892

Bunnell, George C. 1859-1929 - Laura E. 1868-1956 s/s

Lair, Samuel S. died September 14, 1870 - age 30-9-4

Catharine B. daughter of S. S. & R. A. died August 17, 1870 - age 4 month 17 days

Bunnell, James R. born June 22, 1896, died October 10, 1896 - Susie M. born September 6, 1897 died November 9, 1897 s/s Child of C. C. & L. E.

Emrick, Mary Jane wife of Wm. Died May 18, 1868 - age 29-4-12

Garland, John G. son of Daniel & Lucinda died July 16, 1863 - age 2-4-

21

Dunn, John died August 20, 1860 - age 45 years

Bolinger, John died December 20, 1881 - age 75 years

Gift, Elmer E. L. son of W. H. & E. died October 17, 1864 - age 11 months, 15 days

Hugh, Wm. H. son of Uriah & Mary A. Died August 5, 18(9?)5 - age 4-11-22

Strobel, Andrew G. died April 22, 1881 - age 67-2-22 - Lilly (Wife) born Montgomery County,

>Ohio March 17, 1822 died March 23, 1876 - age 54 years 6 days

>Levi son of A. G. & Delilah died December 5, 1860 - age 1 month 12 days

>Mary E. daughter of A. G. ^ D. died May 1, 1860 - age 1-1-26

>Infant daughter died October 9, 1858

>John W. son of A. & L. died July 31, 1874 - Age 22-1-7

Henninger, Luella daughter of J. & M. died January 22, 1883 - age 11 months 2 days

Gebelein, Christiane Marie ehegatten des Karl Gebelein born March 26, 1824 died September 2, 1876

>Johann Heinrich Birnstiel son of Karl born June 26, 1855 died October 24, 1867

Long, Sarah A. daughter of D. K. & B. died August 11, 1855 - age 1 year 11 days

>Infant daughter died July 22, 1870

Oliver, _____ died November 20, 1866 - age 38 years

Collins, Iva 1887-1961 - Samuel 1847-1925 - Rebecca 1847-1927 s/s

Selby, Martha daughter of M. & L. died May 30, 1863 - age 1-8-4

Bechtol, Sarah wife of Daniel born May 10, 1836 died November 12,

1880

    Mary E. daughter of D. & S. died October 7, 1874 - age 11-9-19

    Daniel died May 24, 1896 - age 63-1-14

McClain, Nelson son of A. & M. A. died November 26, 1871 - age 10 days

    Nelson born July 3, 1807 died January 14, 1884 - age 76-6-11

    Amanda wife of Nelson born January 24, 1812 died August 2, 1877 - age 65-6-8

Horner, Analaura daughter of P. & M. A. died July 16, 1864 - age 4-6-27

Hulse, Ida daughter of G. C. & S. C. died June 18, 1864 - age 10 months 7 days

Albrecht, Mary wife of G. W. died April 19, 1857 - age cemented underground

Auer, Joseph died July 21, 1855 - age 22 years 6 months

    Stone initials "W. W."

Henninger, George son of H. & R. died November 16, 1856 - age 24-1-7

    Frederick son of H. & R. died January 16, 1857 - age 22-1-6

    Fridaricker daughter of H. & R. died September 10, 1858 - age 7-5-3

Scheiding, Albert H. 1865-1867 - Charles A. 1870-1871 - Louis J. 1880-1880 s/s

    Stone unreadable except for 20 days

Anderson, James died March 25, 1868 - age 77 years 9 months

    John D. died May 30 1869 - age 77 years 9 months

    Maggie wife of John died August 26, 1895 in her 73rd year

Black, Emma Jane daughter of J. & C. died September 25, 18?? - age 1 month 25 days

Albright, Glendela daughter of P. H. & C. died February 6, 1867 - age 6 months 6 days

Eichelbarger, Louisa died July 4, 1913 - age 71-6-24

Joseph died July 28, 1856 - age 49-3-16 (Father)

Elizabeth died September 18, 1893 - age 86-5-6 (Mother)

Elizabeth wife of Fredrick died August 22, 1854 - 75 year of her age

Eliza A. died January 1, 1894 - age 68 years 19 days (Mother)

Henry L. died December 31, 1863 - age 36-2-16 (Father)

Albright, Susan McLaine daughter of Isaac & Mary died October 10, 1852 - age 1-9-17

Eichelberger, Martha E. died April 17, 1914 - age 55-6-12

Michael, Margaret wife of Wm. Died March 1855 - age 74 years

William D. died October 1855 - age 100 years 4 months
Revolutionary War

Reed, Joseph - Company B, 110 Regiment OVI born March 6, 1831 died December 23, 1889

G. A. R.

Marie P. born April 17, 1846 died February 18, 1920 s/s

Susan died August 1, 1892 - age 67-1-8

Bonham, Sarah daughter of U. & S. died July 6, 1860 - age 3 months 12 days

Ambrose son of U. & S. died August 25, 1862 - age 5 months

Uriah S. died February 11, 1886 - age 64-2-10

Susan wife of Uriah S. died November 15, 1866 - age 31-3-24 s/s

Snyder, Peter died April 20, 1862 - age 73-5-14

McElwaine, Alpheus born June 16, 1835 died September 3, 1911

Elizabeth A. wife of A. died February 1, 1875 - age 32-3-17

Edward died October 1, 1886 - age 21-6-28 s/s

John died August 25, 1873 - age 3-10-27 s/s as above

Schnorf, John died February 25, 1863 - age 25-2-15

Joseph died August 1, 1882 age 71-8-18

Sarah died April 5, 1894 - age 84-1-29

Strubel, John born 1842, died July 31, 1874 G. A. R.

Karr, Zeraniah S. son of J & M. died May 11, 1872 - age 27-8-6

John Iser son of J. & M. died October 22, 1860 - age 2-6-22

Rachel Jane died February 1, 1875 - age 22-5-29

Sarah E. daughter of J. & M. died April 13, 1878 - age 18 years 27 days

John died January 14, 1872 - age 56-8-11

Mary wife of John died November 17, 1892 - age 73-4-22 s/s

Gordon, Henry 1825-1914 - Nancy [Owen] 1826-1861 s/s

Philip 1788-1857 - Elizabeth 1782-1863 s/s

Stone with top gone died June 21, 1856 - age 23-8-20

Hardon, Jonathan died April 13, 1863 - age 60-4-11

Diffendal or Biffendall, Elizabeth died November 8, 1861 - age 90-6-23 (broken)

Stone broken and unreadable

Albright, Infant son of P. & ? (No dates)

____? ____? Of ?&? Albright died ?30, 1852 - age 1-1-27

Grau, M. D. Bosina wife of John A. died June 26, 1856 - age 25-2-23

Scheiding, Margaret wife of John 1837-1880 - 2nd stone died March 29, 1880 - age 42-11-8

Grau, G. L. died July 24, 1856 - age 25-5-5

____? ____? ____? Pf Isaac & Sarah ____? Died September 8,

1850

Grau, Catharine daughter of J. J. & ____? Died June 27, 1866 - age 5-9-15

Henninger, George M. born November 19, 1806 died August 17, 1882 - age 77-8-28 (Father)

Mary B. born August 20, 1808 died June 14, 1886 - age 77-9-24 (Mother) s/s

Bonham, Amos died January 25, 1893 - age 74-1-29

Abandoned Cemetery

There is a cemetery on Gordon-Landis Road, south of the State Route 722 Intersection about _ mile. It is on the west side of the road, and is landlocked. But there is a fence that separates two fields which can be followed back to the cemetery. As I recall, there is a natural gas pipeline or a orange utility marker at the fence along the road. The cemetery is at the end of the fence row before you get to Beachler's Creek. It is on the south side of the fence and is overgrown with shrubs, and trees. When I was a boy, Dwight Ressler and I used to go there to hunt rabbits in the winter. At that time, the tombstones were still standing (1940s) and names could be read. I have heard the stones were collected and stacked somewhere. I have not been there to verify this. I do know that this cemetery was established by the members of the *Thomas Meeting House* which was the beginning of the Gordon Methodist Church (see Religion in Gordon).

CPSIA information can be obtained
at www.ICGtesting.com
Printed in the USA
LVHW100829181222
735466LV00028BD/506